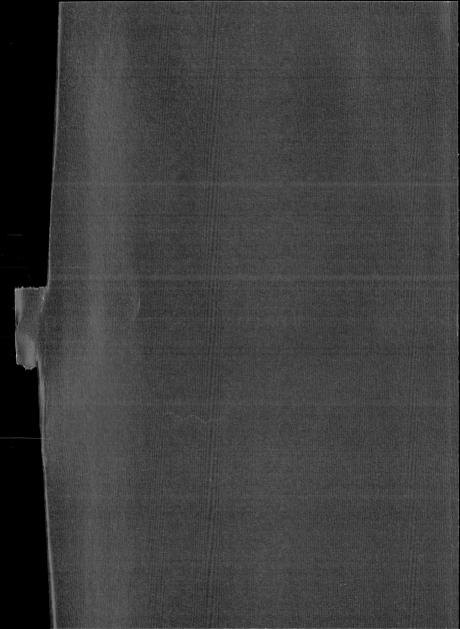

Chocolate
Chocolate
Chocolate

Jean-Pierre Wybauw

ACC EDITIONS

TABLE OF CONTENTS

FOREWORD

Working with chocolate is a pastime, a hobby: discovering ingredients and ideas in order to subsequently surprise yourself. With this book, I aim to inspire as large an audience as possible of chocolate lovers, in order for professionals and aspiring chocolatiers, as well as hobbyists, to find something to their liking.

I made sure that, in addition to a wide range of recipes, all manner of other useful details about chocolate are provided. For example, data about nutritional value constitutes important information for the health conscious. For those who would like to take a look behind the scenes, I will also discuss the origin of cocoa, its history and processing from bean to chocolate.

I hope wholeheartedly that in this book you will rediscover my passion for working with chocolate, and I obviously wish you lots of reading and cooking pleasure!

Jean-

A HEARTFELT THANK YOU

This book was produced with the support and help of a number of people and companies to which I would like to pay tribute.

I owe the most important gratitude of all to my wife, Nelly, who always stood by me patiently and advised and assisted me. For an entire year, we have enthusiastically dedicated every weekend to writing this book together. I would also like to take the opportunity to extend my thanks to:

- my son Walter, who dug up my résumé from his archives;
- Alexandre Bourdeaux, for the production of a number of patisserie recipes;
- Mol d'Art (www.moldart.be), which has contributed to the completion of this project by providing financial support and supplying chocolate melting tubs and hollow figurines;
- Robot-Coupe (www.robot-coupe.be) for making available a Robot-Coupe blender;
- Wine World (www.wineworld.be) for organizing a wine-tasting event with professionals from the wine industry.
- Chocolate World (www.chocolateworld.be);
- and – last but not least – Frank Croes, for his magnificent photographs and excellent team work.

Jean-Pierre Wybauw

MASTER CHOCOLATIER
JEAN-PIERRE WYBAUW

Jean-Pierre Wybauw is respected worldwide as a consultant in chocolate and confectionery. In addition to numerous contributions to culinary magazines, he has also authored a number of books: *Fine Chocolates: Great Experience* (2007), *Chocolate without Borders* (2007), *Chocolate Decorations* (2007), *Fine Chocolates 2: Ganache* (2008) and *Fine Chocolates 3: Extending Shelf Life* (2010). In these works, he shares his many years of experience and his passion for chocolate with professionals and lovers of the world's most popular delicacy.

Jean-Pierre graduated from the Centre for Education and Research for the Food Industry (COOVI-CERIA) in Brussels in 1960. Subsequently, he studied "decoration techniques, desserts and marzipan figurines" at the Provincial Institute for the Food Industry, Antwerp (PIVA).

After his studies, he started working for Patisserie Willems in Antwerp. One year later, he was appointed as head of the design department at the renowned Del Rey confectioners. But he had teaching in his blood and, in 1965, he became a full-time chocolate and confectionery instructor at COOVI-CERIA in Brussels.

His boundless creativity and his love for drawing and painting led him to use silk-screening techniques for the decoration of chocolate. In 1965, he devised the first foils to print on chocolate. This technique is now used throughout the world to apply fine decorations on chocolates and chocolate figurines (see *Transfer sheets* on page 175).

In 1972, Jean-Pierre began working as a technical adviser in the chocolate industry. Since then, he has been giving lessons, lectures and demonstrations across the globe in chocolate processing and he is a regular guest at trade fairs. He frequently hosts workshops for professionals at famous schools in Germany, Japan, Australia, the USA and elsewhere.

In 2002, he was awarded the coveted title of "Chef of the Year" by the Culinary Institute of America in New York. In 2006, his book *Fine Chocolates: Great Experience* (2007) (*Perfecte Pralines* (2004)) won the Golden Ladle at the Australian World Food Media Awards in the "Best Professional Cookery Book" category. The book has since been translated into seven languages, with the French and English editions winning first prize in the "Best Chocolate Book in the World" category at the Gourmand World Cookbook Awards in Malaysia.

Jean-Pierre is a regular guest on a number of culinary programs on radio and TV globally, and is also a member of the jury of various international professional culinary competitions. For example, at the biannual World Pastry Team Championships (WPTCs) in Beaver Creek, Colorado, Las Vegas, Nevada, and Phoenix, Arizona, his opinion has always been highly valued.

It is with enthusiasm and never-ceasing diligence that he perfected the processing of chocolate, which has led to this new publication. *Chocolate Chocolate Chocolate* is the sixth book with which Jean-Pierre Wybauw makes a half century of knowledge and experience accessible to a larger audience.

WHAT IS CHOCOLATE
AND WHAT IS IT ACTUALLY MADE OF?

We know chocolate as a solid, hard, smoothly melting and glossy delicacy. In addition, this source of delight, enjoyed by practically everyone, has numerous applications. It is not only "just" consumed as chocolate, but is also used in the preparation of desserts, pastries and drinks, and it has even found its way into the kitchen.

There are three basic varieties: dark, milk and white chocolate. But which raw materials are they actually made up of?

Dark chocolate is produced by processing and mixing cocoa beans, sugar and vanilla (or vanillin) (see page 179). At the end of the process, additional cocoa butter is typically added (from the cocoa beans) as well as lecithin (from soya beans). The addition of extra cocoa butter liquefies the chocolate even further, which is necessary for a number of applications. This makes the chocolate in its hard form even harder, resulting in a more pleasant snap and allowing for a thinner coating on biscuits and chocolates. Soya lecithin is required to stabilize the emulsion and increase the liquidity of the chocolate (see page 118).

The proportion of ingredients determines the flavor of the end product, which can vary from extra bitter and semi-bitter to semi-sweet and sweet.

The ingredients for *milk chocolate* are cocoa beans, sugar, milk powder and natural vanilla (or vanillin, for cheaper chocolates). Here, too, the proportions play a major role, as they can either result in an intensely cocoa-flavored milk chocolate, or a rather creamy milk chocolate or even a chocolate with a predominately caramel-like aroma. The latter is the result of some milk powders combined with the sugar giving off a typical caramel flavor during the production process.

White chocolate is different from dark and milk chocolate since no dry cocoa bean components are used in its preparation. The ingredients for white chocolate include cocoa butter, sugar, milk powder, lecithin and natural vanilla (or vanillin). Here, again, the flavor is primarily determined by the proportion of ingredients, which produce a sweet, creamy or caramel-like end product.

Block, *baking* or *household chocolate* contains at least 30% dry cocoa components.

Semi-bitter chocolate contains at least 43% dry cocoa components.

Bitter chocolate contains at least 60% dry cocoa components.

Couverture

For the creation of figurines, chocolates and small decorations, it is best to use *couverture*, which is easier to process due to its high cocoa butter content. It is harder with better shrinkage (see page 140), making it easier to unmold shapes. Couverture is richer in flavor than regular chocolate with less cocoa butter, since cocoa butter retains flavors longer.

The term "couverture" is legally protected and may only be used for chocolate with a total fat content of at least 31%.

For darker chocolate, this implies at least 31% cocoa butter; for milk chocolate, at least a total

fat content (cocoa butter + milk fat) of 31%; white chocolate may not be referred to as couverture.

The label couverture is an indication of the quality of the chocolate. Due to the higher cocoa butter content, this chocolate will melt more easily in the mouth. It is more liquid, which makes it easier to process and makes dipped chocolates more attractive.

Chocolate without added sugars
The claim that no sugars are added to chocolate is only allowed if no mono- or disaccharides or other foodstuffs used for their sweetening power have been added to the product.

Lactose-free chocolate
This is chocolate made without milk sugar (lactose).

Flavored chocolate
Some chocolates are enhanced with flavors such as mocha, caramel, cappuccino, honey, etc.

Mixing

The cocoa beans – sourced from a number of countries and each with its specific flavor and aroma – are mixed in accordance with specific recipes in order to produce a previously determined flavor profile and an identical, consistent flavor. For so-called *chocolate of origin*, beans are sourced from a single country or origin.

Cleaning, breaking, roasting and removing bacteria

The cocoa beans are thoroughly cleaned and small stones, dust, sand, etc., are removed. Subsequently, they are briefly infrared heated. In this way, they can be more easily broken into irregular pieces, allowing the skin around the beans to be removed. These chunks are referred to as *nibs* (see page 144). The nibs are subsequently roasted, thus developing their typical cocoa flavor.

Grinding

The nibs are further processed in special mills into a liquid mass, i.e., the cocoa mass, which represents the main ingredient in the preparation of chocolate.

Mixing, rolling and conching

First, the various ingredients are weighed in accordance with the recipe:

- for dark chocolate: cocoa mass + cocoa butter + sugar + vanilla
- for milk chocolate: cocoa mass + cocoa butter + sugar + vanilla
- for white chocolate: cocoa butter + sugar + milk powder + vanilla.

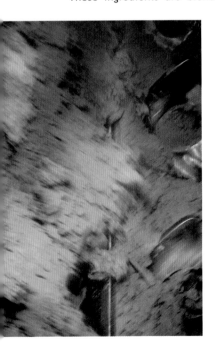

These ingredients are blended together into a homogeneous chocolate mixture, which is crushed into a very fine powder, with particles smaller than the tongue can detect. This gives the finished chocolate that typical unctuous, smooth texture and consistent flavor.

The chocolate powder is subsequently kneaded for several hours in *conches at a high temperature*. Conches are large vessels fitted with powerful agitators on the inside in which the chocolate mixture is kneaded. The air that is constantly injected into the chocolate and the heat released by the kneading result in a number of chemical and physical reactions:

- the last remaining moisture still present in the mixture evaporates
- the cocoa butter (and any milk fats in the preparation of milk or white chocolate) melt
- any remaining sharp edges on the sugar particles are removed
- the volatile acids disappear fully or partially – depending on the conching time – which guarantees the pleasant, refined flavor of the chocolate
- the heat created in the conche results in a kind of caramelizing process, which also contributes to the rich flavor, especially in milk and white chocolate.

Conching is one of the most difficult aspects of the entire production process, and requires a lot of expertise and constant monitoring. At the end of the conching process, some additional cocoa butter and soya lecithin are added as emulsifiers. The quantity of cocoa butter and lecithin affects the viscosity (fluidity) of the chocolate: the more cocoa butter is added, the more fluid the chocolate will become. This is especially important for chocolatiers. If the liquid is too thick, the chocolate layer covering the confections will be too thick and holes may develop on the surface.

The quality of chocolate is determined by so many different factors:

- type of cocoa beans
- quality and freshness of the ingredients
- proportion of the ingredients
- roasting
- refining
- conching
- correct packaging
- correct storage.

Type of cocoa beans

The choice and mixture of the beans play an important role: each cocoa variety has its own specific aromatic properties. African cocoa varieties give chocolate its typical body, its recognizable basic aromas. Asian or Central American cocoa varieties often have more subtle aromas evoking spices, fruit or even flowers.

The type of cocoa tree, the soil on which it is cultivated and climate conditions in part determine the eventual flavor of the cocoa. In order to create chocolate with a consistent flavor, cocoas of various origins are typically mixed until they achieve the correct flavor profile.

There are three basic varieties of cocoa trees: the Criollo, the Forastero and the Trinitario. Their descendants on the plantations are often (intended or accidental) hybrids, each with their own, specific properties. The *Criollo* produces fruits with a very thin skin. The cocoa

itself is pale in color and has unique, refined aromas. This variety is found primarily in Central America and Asia. The Criollo is quite vulnerable and only produces small harvests.

The *Forastero* is a stronger tree variety that is easier to cultivate and produces greater yields. The cocoa fruits have a thicker skin and a coarser, stronger aroma. Trees grown on the basis of Forastero genes are primarily found in Africa. This cocoa gives its typical, recognizable basic aroma to the chocolate and represents up to 80% of the cocoa mixture in most chocolates. Other cocoa varieties are mixed with the Forastero in order to enrich the chocolate with finer, more subtle notes.

The *Trinitario* is a cross between the Criollo and the Forastero and therefore borrows properties from both tree species. The beans from this tree produce a strong, yet fine aroma.

Quality and freshness of the ingredients

In their countries of origin, the cocoa beans undergo a fermentation process, after which they are dried and subsequently shipped to the location where they will be processed into chocolate. As a result of the fermentation and drying method, often all manner of junk ends up between the beans. For example, utensils are regularly found, as well as stones, sand or wood chips. That is why the beans must always be cleaned thoroughly before the production process.

Proportion of the ingredients

The proportion of the ingredients plays a major role: for example, dark chocolate can contain from 40% to more than 70% of cocoa components. That percentage tells us something about the flavor of the chocolate, which can vary from sweet, through semi-bitter to extra bitter.

Roasting

In its dried form, cocoa does not yet have that typical cocoa flavor. To this end, the beans, just like coffee beans, have to be heated in order to change flavor. Roasting time and temperature are of the utmost importance.

The development of aroma in cocoa is an extremely complex process. During roasting, various reactions are created, which lead to a few hundred end products, each playing their own role in the creation of the eventual cocoa aroma.

An important series of processes that occur when cocoa is heated are referred to as the Maillard reaction or non-enzymatic browning,

and also produce flavor and aroma components, which, through chemical conversion, can further develop into highly diverse end products.

Refining

Chocolate components are thoroughly refined so that we do not taste individual particles when eating chocolate. For adequate chocolate, the particles must be smaller than 20 μm (twenty thousandths of a millimeter, or 0.000787 inch). If the particles are larger, we experience chocolate as "gritty".

Conching

Conching (kneading) determines the eventual fine flavor of chocolate. The volatile acids and the last residual moisture, which are originally present in the cocoa, disappear. Conching time is very important, and with modern equipment should not take too long, as this could lead to loss of quality.

Correct packaging

Due to exposure to light and air, chocolate will quickly lose its pleasant aroma and flavor. That is why chocolate should always be carefully packaged. White chocolate is the most sensitive and oxidizes quickly when exposed to light and air, turning it white (white chocolate should be yellow). Therefore, chocolate should never be exposed to cigarette smoke, refrigerator odors, packaging smelling like cardboard, etc.

Correct storage

In order to preserve chocolate for a long time, it must be packaged properly and stored airtight away from sunlight in an odorless, cool and dry place. The ideal temperature is below 65°F/18°C. If the chocolate is packaged correctly, it can be kept in the refrigerator without problems. When cold chocolate (e.g., out of the refrigerator) is removed from its packaging in a warm environment, condensation moisture will form on the surface of the chocolate. As a result, this chocolate will therefore be somewhat less glossy, but there is no loss of quality.

TRENDS IN CHOCOLATES

Flavor

Why is it that flavors evolve? What happened to the traditional vanilla, mocha, pistachio, banana and cinnamon favorites? And why is it that orange blossom water, which used to be routinely integrated into all manner of desserts and especially in marzipan, has now practically disappeared?

All kinds of spices from faraway countries are becoming popular. Spices that used to be little known or unknown in the Western world, such as cardamom, tonka, green tea, wasabi, mahleb and so many others, are now in. This is, of course, a result of increased travel and distances no longer being an issue. People are getting to know and appreciate new flavors in exotic locations and bring this flavor culture back to their regions.

Better professionals are also getting increasingly creative. Their technical knowledge of ingredients is expanding, thus encouraging innovation. In addition, quality and originality are important when faced with the competition.

Structure

An evolution is also ongoing in the area of the structure of the creams. Belgian chocolates have been a favorite for a long time for their buttery and smooth creams. In Germany, Switzerland and Austria, on the other hand, we find a lot of solid fillings, consisting of praline, marzipan, nut products or fondant with fruit flavors. Heavy fillings are slowly being

replaced by ganache chocolates, which clearly contain less fat and better balanced aromas. Due to their high moisture content, these creams are much lighter and feel softer in the mouth. A refined assortment today is primarily made up of ganache chocolates. Furthermore, consumers are more health conscious, hence the trend to reduce sugar, resulting in the chocolate's stronger cocoa flavor.

Outside

Even the outside of chocolates is subject to changes. For many years, Belgium and the Netherlands have been trendsetters for molded chocolates, while the French predominantly produce dipped chocolates.

Dimensions and weight

True to tradition, the dimensions of chocolates vary from country to country. Even though the Dutch are increasingly attempting to match Belgian chocolates with respect to size, compared to other countries, the Dutch take the cake, as it were, with their huge chocolates. Greek consumers increasingly request very large chocolates, which are typically referred to as *"bouchées"*.

Belgian chocolates range between 0.35 and 0.45 oz (11 and 14 grams), with a number of exceptions at ¾ oz (20 g). However, the trend towards smaller chocolates continues among better chocolatiers in Belgium. This involves chocolates with an average weight of 0.26 or 0.29 oz (8 or 9 grams), as is the case in Switzerland and France, where smaller chocolates are routinely produced.

Personally, I prefer enjoying two different small chocolates than a single one that fills your entire mouth. For that matter, a 2.2-lb (1-kg) *"ballotin"* (see page 58) with an average of 125 pieces is more attractive than one with only 70 to 90 pieces, as is the case for traditional Belgian chocolates.

In this table, we provide the average nutritional values per 3½ oz (100 g) of quality chocolate.

	Dark chocolate	Milk chocolate	White chocolate
Energy (kilocalories)	535 kcal	561 kcal	571 kcal
Energy (kilojoules)	2,236 kJ	2,347 kJ	2,388 kJ
Total protein	5 g	7 g	6 g
Milk protein	0 g	5.7 g	6 g
Vitamin B5 (RDA)	5.8%	14.2%	13.3%
Vitamin B6 (pyridoxine)	0.0 mg	0.1 mg	0.1 mg
Vitamin B6 (RDA)	2.2%	3.9%	3.5%
Vitamin B12 (cyanocobalamin)	0.0 μg	0.5 μg	0.5 μg
Vitamin B12 (RDA)	0.0%	47.0%	49.4%
Total carbohydrates	46.8 g	51.4 g	55.5 g
Sugars (mono- and disaccharides)	43.9 g	50.4 g	55.1 g
Starch	2.4 g	0.6 g	0.0 g
Total fat	36.1 g	36.2 g	36.0 g
Saturated fat	22.6 g	22.9 g	22.8 g
Monounsaturated fat	12.7 g	12.5 g	12.4 g
Polyunsaturated fat	0.8 g	0.8 g	0.8 g
Total trans fatty acids	0.0 g	0.4 g	0.4 g
Cholesterol	1.0 mg	22.5 mg	23.6 mg

Organic acids	0.65 g	0.53 g	0.38 g
Fiber	7.2 g	1.9 g	0.0 g
Total alkaloids	0.7 g	0.2 g	0.0 g
Vitamin A (retinol)	15 μg	64 μg	66 μg
Polyhydroxy phenol	1.3 g	0.3 g	0.0 g
Vitamin A (RDA)	1.8%	7.6%	7.9%
Vitamin A (IU)	51	212	220
Provitamin A (beta-carotene)	0 μg	5 μg	5 μg
Vitamin B1 (thiamine)	0.1 mg	0.1 mg	0.1 mg
Vitamin B1 (RDA)	0.0%	0.0%	0.0%
Vitamin B2 (riboflavin)	0.1 mg	0.5 mg	0.5 mg
Vitamin B2 (RDA)	5.5%	30.8%	30.9%
Vitamin B3 (niacin)	0.7 mg	0.2 mg	0.0 mg
Vitamin B3 (RDA)	3.6%	0.9%	0.0%
Vitamin B5 (pantothenic acid)	0.4 mg	0.9 mg	0.8 mg
Vitamin C (ascorbic acid)	0.0 mg	0.4 mg	0.4 mg
Vitamin C (RDA)	0%	0.7%	0.7%
Vitamin D (calciferol)	1.7 μg	1.3 μg	1.3 μg
Vitamin D (RDA)	34.1%	26.8%	26.5%
Vitamin D (IU)	6.8	5.4	5.3
Vitamin E (alpha-tocopherol)	3.1 mg	2.4 mg	2.4 mg
Vitamin E (RDA)	30.8%	24.2%	23.9%
Vitamin E (IU)	2.1	1.6	1.6
Vitamin M (folic acid)	11.5 μg	10.6 μg	9.2 μg
Sodium	4.4 mg	82.1 mg	85.2 mg
Phosphorus	161.8 mg	210.9 mg	177.9 mg
Phosphorus (RDA)	20.2%	26.4%	22.2%

Iron	3.2 mg	1.0 mg	0.3 mg
Iron (RDA)	22.7%	7.3%	1.8%
Magnesium	102.2 mg	44.9 mg	19.5 mg
Magnesium (RDA)	34.1%	15.0%	6.5%
Zinc	1.4 mg	1.1 mg	0.8 mg
Zinc (RDA)	9.6%	7.4%	5.2%
Iodine	0.0 μg	6 μg	6 μg
Iodine (RDA)	0.0%	3.9%	4.1%
Calcium	28.4 mg	206.4 mg	209.5 mg
Calcium (RDA)	3.6%	25.8%	26.2%
Chlorine	8.6 mg	179.2 mg	186.4 mg
Potassium	590.3 mg	414.3 mg	305.8 mg
Ash content	1.5 g	1.9 g	1.7 g

Acronyms

IU = international units

RDA = recommended daily allowance (expressed as a percentage)

THE SUCCESS
OF BELGIAN CHOCOLATES

The fact that Belgian chocolates are so successful worldwide can be attributed to a number of factors.

Belgium was one of the first countries where the industrialization of chocolate led to highly refined chocolate. The Belgians pride themselves on a number of large chocolate factories located in Belgium. They produce a wide array of types and flavors. There is enormous variety: in some factories, 1½ tons (1,500 kg) of chocolate are produced every two minutes, and this around the clock.

Obviously our Belgian *chocolatiers* and *patissiers* also played a major role in the advance of "Belgian chocolates". For decades, they have been creating chocolates that are enjoyed by both young and old and that are loved because of their mildly sweet, recognizable flavor profile on the basis of ganache, praline, gianduja (which features hazelnuts), fruits and liqueurs, etc.

And… molded and filled chocolates were born in Belgium in 1912. *Jean Neuhaus* was the first to produce chocolate shells, which he would later fill with cream.

The last factor is price. Belgium is known for excellent *value for money*, in both chocolate and "pralines".

Because cocoa naturally contains substances that promote shelf life, chocolate can be kept for a very long time, provided it is handled correctly.

Always keep chocolate in a dark, dry and cool place, protected from air, in odorless packaging.

This allows dark chocolate to be kept for up to two years, milk chocolate up to 18 months and white chocolate up to one year. It is impossible to provide an average shelf life for chocolates, since it totally depends on the other ingredients, such as moisture and fat.

If chocolate is not kept correctly, various forms of deterioration can occur:
- chemical deterioration
- microbial deterioration
- physical deterioration.

These processes are often combined or successive.

Chemical deterioration

The principal form of chemical deterioration in chocolate products is fat oxidation.

A distinction must be made between oxidative rancidity and hydrolytic rancidity (saponification).

Oxidative rancidity   After long-term exposure to air and light, chocolate will lose its pleasant flavor and aroma. A common example is the oxidation of white chocolate under the influence of light. The chocolate turns snow white and acquires a typical oxidation flavor. Discoloration is the result of the oxidation of the natural dyes present in cocoa butter. Oxidation of white chocolate can be avoided by minimizing the product's exposure to light.

Conditions for oxidative rancidity are the presence of unsaturated fatty acids and oxygen. This type of oxidation is introduced by light, trace metal, heat and specific enzymes. Finished chocolates should be packaged as soon as possible.

Cocoa contains natural antioxidants (polyhydroxy phenols), which protect cocoa butter against oxidation. When pressing cocoa mass into cocoa powder and cocoa butter, the polyhydroxy phenols remain in powdered fraction. That is why white chocolate is not protected against oxidative rancidity, in contrast with milk chocolate and, more particularly, dark chocolate.

Hydrolytic rancidity (saponification)   The first condition for hydrolytic rancidity is the presence of lipases. These lipases (catalysts) are primarily of microbial origin. They can either be present as such in the ingredients or created through microbial growth in the chocolate product.

The second condition is the presence of a certain amount of moisture. A typical example of this form of deterioration is therefore the development of a soapy flavor in fillings with relatively high moisture content.

Microbial deterioration

Microbial deterioration is, as the name suggests, caused by *micro-organisms*. These can be molds, yeasts or bacteria, which end up in the product through the ingredients, the environment, machines or personnel. A few examples of microbial deterioration are the following:

- fungal growth on the contact surface between center and chocolate shell
- bursting chocolates due to gas formation; osmophile yeasts convert sugars into CO_2 gas
- the curdling of cream fillings; lactic acid bacteria convert sugars into organic acids (to be noted is that this form of deterioration only makes the product unpleasant, but it has no other medical side-effects).

Not a single food product is free from micro-organisms, as a number of germs are always present. That is why it is important to keep the conditions so that the existing organisms are unable to multiply and spoil the product. Depending on the types of organisms, they require water and/or *food products* (sugars, fats, protein, oxygen) to develop. Many micro-organisms require oxygen, which is why it is not always sufficient to vacuum the fillings to prevent them from multiplying.

Temperature has a clear impact on the multiplication speed and activity of micro-organisms. The optimum growth temperature for many micro-organisms varies between 75°F and 105°F (25°C and 40°C). Refrigerator temperatures do slow down the growth of micro-organisms, but only deep freeze temperatures stop all microbial processes. Good preservation temperatures for chocolate products range between 50°F and 70°F (10°C and 20°C), but only curb the growth of micro-organisms, at best.

The quantity of available *water* is a very important factor in microbial deterioration and is obviously highly dependent on moisture content, but also on the nature of the other substances. The majority of ganache recipes contain quite a lot of water from the ingredients, since water provides the ganache with its pleasant, creamy, smooth and light structure. It is therefore a fact that water is the culture medium for numerous micro-organisms such as fungi, yeasts and dangerous bacteria (e.g., salmonella and listeria). Numerous ingredients, such as cream, milk, butter, pure fruit juice or fruit pulp, etc., are primarily made up of water. The total moisture content of a recipe only provides limited information on its shelf life. Shelf life actually depends on the quantity of water available to micro-organisms as well as on chemical reactions.

Physical deterioration

Highly diverse phenomena fall under this designation: sugarbloom, fatbloom, fat migration, absorption of strange odors, loss of aroma.

Sugarbloom   Sugarbloom is the phenomenon whereby the chocolate surface becomes grainy and white. It is different from fatbloom insofar as sugarbloom feels coarse and does not disappear when touched. The reason for sugarbloom is moisture condensation on the chocolate surface.

The sugar in the chocolate dissolves in the condensed moisture and, when the water evaporates, the sugar crystallizes on the chocolate surface. The only way to prevent it is to avoid condensation by keeping the moisture content in the air low, or by avoiding major temperature fluctuations (not cooling the products too long – or keeping them in a refrigerator that is too humid).

Fatbloom   Fatbloom can be recognized from a gray film on the chocolate surface. Just as in sugarbloom, the chocolate looks old. Fatbloom is created by the recrystallization of the fat on the chocolate surface.

Fat migration   Fat migration refers to the transfer of specific liquid fat fractions from the ganache to the chocolate layer. Fat migration can lead to the chocolate softening and producing fatbloom.

Absorption of odors   The last deterioration category is the absorption of foreign odors by the chocolate. Some flavor contaminations (e.g., spices) and aromas seem obvious. Other flavor and odor issues are not that easy to identify. In most cases, the reason is a specific organic molecule, which is absorbed from the environment through direct contact (e.g., with the packaging) or through the surrounding air. In the last few years, an increasing number of chemical compounds have been discovered that, in some cases, can contaminate entire loads of food products, resulting in major losses and expenses.

Cooking with chocolate   Weight measurements are listed as metric units, as per Chef Wybauw's original tried-and-tested recipes, alongside imperial and American system equivalents. The metric to imperial conversions featured throughout this book are approximate and represent equivalent measurements rather than exact conversions.

A kitchen scale, as well as measuring cups and spoons, will help to provide accurate conversions between the different systems of measurements. There are also a number of excellent conversion charts and calculators available online and in most standard cookbooks.

The suggested oven temperatures and cooking times may vary from oven to oven. Oven temperatures originally expressed as Celsius units have been converted and rounded up or down to the nearest five degrees Fahrenheit.

RECIPES AND TERMINOLOGY

Anise ganache

Ingredients
12 oz (350 g) cream • ⅛ oz (5 g) dried anise (aniseed) seeds • 4½ oz (130 g) butter • 2¾ oz (80 g) honey • 1 lb 2 oz (500 g) dark chocolate • granulated sugar

Method
Bring the cream, anise seeds, honey and butter to a boil.
Leave to infuse until the cream is completely cooled.
Strain the cream and pour onto the tempered chocolate at approximately 85°F/30°C, mix thoroughly and pipe the ganache into long strips using a pastry bag fitted with a smooth tip.
Leave to crystallize sufficiently before dipping into dark chocolate.
Roll into granulated sugar to finish.

Antioxidants

The human body is constantly being attacked by *oxidants* or free radicals. Oxidants are unstable molecules, which can harm healthy tissues, resulting in infections. Fortunately, the body also produces so-called "antioxidants". These molecules are present in the body primarily to neutralize unstable molecules, before they can do any harm. It is still recommended to lend nature a helping hand by eating food containing antioxidants. Specific vitamins, for example, act as antioxidants (such as vitamin C), but other substances also fulfill this function in the body, such as polyphenols, which can primarily be found in green tea, dark chocolate and wine.

The beneficial effects of (dark) chocolate are therefore attributed to its natural high polyphenol content (i.e., catechine and procyanids, whether or not linked to protein). These components are classified under antioxidants, which, in a manner of speaking, detoxify the body, thereby contributing to healthy heart and blood vessels.

Apricot pie

Ingredients for chocolate crumble pastry
5½ oz (150 g) butter • 5 oz (140 g) powdered sugar • 1¾ oz (50 g) egg • 1 oz (30 g) almond powder • 7½ oz (210 g) flour • ¹⁄₁₆ oz (2 g) baking powder • 1½ oz (40 g) cocoa powder • ¹⁄₁₆ oz (2 g) salt

Method for chocolate crumble pastry
Whip the butter and the sugar into a cream. Add the egg and almond powder.
Sift the flour, baking powder, cocoa and salt, and fold into the butter.
Allow to rest for approximately 2 hours in the refrigerator.
Roll the dough out to about ⅛ inch (2.5 mm) and line a pie mold.
Puncture the dough in order to prevent air bubbles.
Bake for approximately 15 minutes in a 340°F/170°C oven.

Ingredients for filling
3½ oz (100 g butter) • 3½ oz (100 g) powdered sugar • 2¾ oz (80 g)
egg • 3½ oz (100 g) almond powder • ½ oz (15 g) cocoa powder •
apricot pulp • half apricots • almond slivers

Method for filling
Blend the butter and sugar into a cream, add the egg with the
almond and cocoa powders.
Leave this almond paste to rest in the refrigerator for approximately
two hours.
Spread the apricot pulp on the bottom and fill the crust with almond
paste to approximately ¼ inch (5 mm) from the rim.
Cut apricots in half and arrange them on the almond paste.
Decorate with almond slivers.
Bake in a 340°F/170°C oven for approximately 35 minutes.

Arabe

Ingredients
3½ oz (100 g) pistachio nuts • 3½ oz (100 g) marzipan • 3½ oz (100 g)
cassis liqueur (crème de cassis) • 7 oz (200 g) honey • 10½ oz (300 g)
butter • 1 lb 12 oz (800 g) milk chocolate

Method
Grind the pistachio nuts into a fine powder.
Add the marzipan and blackcurrant liqueur and mix thoroughly.
Blend in the honey and butter and beat into a smooth cream.

Lastly, fold in the chocolate.

Fill a chocolate mold with dark chocolate. Pipe the cream into the molds using a pastry bag. Allow the filling to slightly set before spreading the dark chocolate in the mold.

The Aztecs

The history of cocoa takes us back to the Aztecs. The cocoa bean is said to have originated in northern South America, in the Amazon area, among others. In Central America, all cocoa beans were harvested by the Toltecs, a civilized people that lived in central Mexico in the 10th and 11th centuries AD. The Aztecs reclaimed the surroundings of what is currently Mexico City from the Toltecs. Originally, they used cocoa beans as currency and subsequently also as a stimulant. They peeled the beans, ground them and mixed them with spices and honey to improve the flavor.

Baba with chocolate

Ingredients
4½ oz (125 g) flour · ½ oz (15 g) cocoa butter (softened) · ¼ oz (10 g) baker's yeast · ¾ oz (20 g) sugar · ¹⁄₁₆ oz (3 g) salt · 2 eggs · 1¾ oz (50 g) water · 1¾ oz (50 g) butter (melted)

Method

Strain the flour into the softened cocoa butter and place in the food processor.

Knead the yeast, sugar, salt and eggs. Then add the water and melted butter. Cover the dough and leave to rest for some 30 minutes.

Briefly knead the dough again.

Pipe the dough into baba molds or half-shere shaped non-stick molds. Allow the dough to rise in a heated environment.

Bake the babas for 35 minutes in the oven at approximately 340°F/170°C.

Ingredients for the dip

Apricot or other fruit pulp

Method for dip

Pour the fruit pulp into the food processor and puree into a thick paste.

Bring the puree to a boil and dilute into a syrup by adding water.

Strain the syrup into a bowl (jam can also be used as an alternative).

Dip the babas into this syrup and make sure they are thoroughly saturated. Then place them on a rack to drain.

Arrange the babas on a serving dish. Garnish with fruit and cover with a little chocolate sauce (see *Diplomat with chocolate sauce* recipe on page 89).

"Ballotin"

The famous cardboard box in which the chocolates are so neatly arranged is said to be an invention of Jean Neuhaus. Chocolates used to be sold in cone-shaped bags, resulting in the bottom chocolates usually getting crushed. In 1915, this led Neuhaus to produce a cardboard box. This Belgian invention can now be found across the globe.

Baumé

Antoine Baumé, a French physicist who lived from 1728 to 1804, developed the hydrometer, a device to determine the specific gravity of liquids, which is referred to as sugar scale, density meter or Baumé meter. The degrees on the scale bear his name (°B).

Whenever we heat a sugar syrup, water evaporates, resulting in the specific gravity of the syrup increasing and the Baumé meter sinking less deeply into the syrup. The scale on the Baumé meter ranges from 0°B – in 60°F/17°C water – to 50°B.

The syrup's density depends on the temperature. Example: a warm, 33°B sugar syrup will show 36°B in cold conditions and will weigh 3 lb 2¼ oz (1,360 grams).

We can express it as follows:

syrup	>	water content
20°B	>	60%
27°B	>	50%
30°B	>	45%
33°B	>	40%
36°B	>	32%
40°B	>	25%
43°B	>	14%
45°B	>	9%
48°B	>	6.5%

For correct readings, the Baumé meter must be rinsed and dried after each weighing, otherwise the meter will sink in too deeply, weighed down by the adhering sugar, resulting in a distorted figure. The accuracy of the measurement is also determined by the syrup's temperature. Some time ago, the Baumé was used routinely, but it is increasingly being replaced by the more accurate refractometer.

Bavarois

A bavarois or Bavarian cream is a very light and mild cream, which is poured into a mold, cooled and subsequently unmolded. Fruit puree, fruit chunks, praline or chocolate can be added.

Ingredients
½ vanilla pod • 10½ oz (300 g) milk • 3½ oz (100 g) dark chocolate • ¼ oz (10 g) gelatin • 3 egg yolks • 3½ oz (100 g) sugar • 10½ oz (300 g) heavy cream

Method
Scrape the seeds from half a vanilla pod into the milk and add the vanilla pod and the chocolate.
Heat the milk.
Soak the gelatin in water.
Thoroughly beat the egg yolks and the sugar and blend in the warm milk.
Carefully thicken the mass on low heat and add the wrung-out gelatin leaves. Mix thoroughly and pour through a pointed strainer.
Leave to cool. Stir occasionally until the mixture nearly reaches room temperature and fold in the cream beaten into soft peaks.
Pour into a pie mold or into a moistened silicone mold.
Place in the refrigerator until the cream is stiff enough to be unmolded.
Garnish to taste.

Bresilienne (crushed nuts with sugar)

Bresilienne is primarily used for pie crust edges, to garnish chocolates or as a truffle coating. It is made up of small pieces of hazelnuts or almonds, coated with a thin layer of slightly caramelized sugar.

Ingredients
7 oz (200 g) hazelnuts or almonds • 1¾ oz (50 g) water • 9 oz (250 g) sugar • 1¾ oz (50 g) honey

Method
Finely chop the hazelnuts or almonds to the desired size. Bring the sugar and water to a boil.
Add the chopped nuts, heat while stirring until the sugar turns sandy and light brown. Fold in the honey and remove from the heat. Pour the mixture onto a non-stick mat to cool. If necessary, separate the grains. Keep the bresilienne in a container or in a properly sealed jar.

Buche or Yule log

Ingredients for cocoa biscuit
1½ oz (40 g) flour • 1½ oz (40 g) cocoa powder • 2½ oz (70 g) egg yolks • 6 oz (170 g) eggs • 4¾ oz (135 g) sugar • 4 oz (110 g) egg white • 2 oz (55 g) sugar

Method for cocoa biscuit
Sift the flour together with the cocoa powder. Beat the egg yolks,

eggs and sugar into a foam. Separately beat the egg whites and sugar into peaks.

Carefully blend both foams and gently add the flour mixture; stir as little as possible.

Spread a thin layer on a 23½ x 15¾ inch (60 x 40 cm) Silpat (silicone) mat and bake for approximately 10 minutes at 390°F/200°C.

Praliné feuilleté ingredients
5 oz (140 g) milk chocolate · 5¾ oz (165 g) pure hazelnut paste (heavily roasted hazelnuts refined into oil) · 3½ oz (100 g) pailleté feuilletine[1]

Method for praliné feuilleté
Mix the ingredients and spread a thin layer of the mixture on the cooled biscuit. Place the biscuit layer in a frame (or mold).

Anglaise ingredients
9½ oz (260 g) milk · 2¾ oz (80 g) egg yolk · 1¾ oz (50 g) sugar

Method for anglaise
Bring two-thirds of the milk to a boil. Blend the yolks with the sugar and add to the reserved cold milk. Pour the mixture into the boiled milk and stir thoroughly, while heating to 185°F/85°C.

---

[1] Pailleté feuilletine is made up of very thin crunchy biscuit flakes. As an alternative, finely ground cornflakes can be used (cornflakes are much thicker than pailleté feuilletine).

Chocolate mousse ingredients
8 oz (225 g) anglaise · 5¾ oz (160 g) dark chocolate · 11½ oz (320 g)
lightly beaten cream

Working method for chocolate mousse
Mix the anglaise with the melted, room-temperature chocolate and
fold in the cream.

Finishing touches
Pour the mousse into the frame, smooth out and refrigerate.
Using a warm knife, cut into the desired dimensions. Apply very
thin chocolate slivers[2] on and around the log.

Cocoa butter

The difference between fat and oil involves fluidity. Oil is liquid at
room temperature (approximately 70°F/20°C). Fat is solid at room
temperature. Cocoa fruit contains 55% cocoa fat, which becomes
fairly soft and spreadable at body temperature, which is why we
call it cocoa butter. It melts at approximately 97°F/36°C, which
makes cocoa butter ideal for specific cosmetics applications. It is
frequently used in lip balms and skin creams.

Cocoa butter is pressed from cocoa beans. In 1828, Coenraad
Van Houten developed a device that was able to separate the

---

[2] Pour a little chocolate between two sheets of shiny foil and roll out into a very thin layer.
Allow to crystallize thoroughly before removing the foil. Break the chocolate into irregular pieces.

cocoa mass in cocoa butter from the cocoa "cake". The cocoa mass is pumped into large cocoa presses; modern cocoa presses have a pressure of approximately 1000 bar.

Rough cocoa butter, fresh from the cocoa press, still contains approximately 0.5% cocoa powder particles and is therefore light yellowish brown in color. In order to obtain clear cocoa butter, these cocoa particles are separated from the cocoa butter. Subsequently, the butter is deodorized through steam distillation in order to remove odor and flavor.

Butter ganache with cognac

This butter ganache is combined with a layer of marzipan.

Ingredients
marzipan for the crust • 4½ oz (130 g) butter • 4½ oz (130 g) fondant • 9½ oz (270 g) milk chocolate (melted) • 4¼ oz (120 g) cognac • dark chocolate (melted, for decoration)

Method
Roll marzipan into an ⅛-inch (3-mm) layer and place in a frame approximately ½ inch (10 mm) high. Beat the softened butter. Slowly add the fondant and blend into a smooth cream.
Fold in the cooled melted milk chocolate and then the cognac.
Spread the cream on the marzipan in the frame.
Leave to crystallize sufficiently before cutting with a wire slicer or knife.
Dip into dark chocolate (see page 91) and decorate.

Cannelloni with apricot cream

Ingredients
5½ oz (150 g) butter · 1 oz (30 g) invert sugar · 10½ oz (300 g) milk
chocolate · 5½ oz (150 g) apricot puree · 1¾ oz (50 g) cognac

Method
Soften the butter and add the invert sugar and then the tempered
chocolate.
Fold the apricot puree and the cognac into the butter mixture.
Using a pastry bag, pipe out circular strips. Allow to crystallize and
spread the chocolate evenly on all sides using a brush.
Cut the strips as soon as the chocolate has slightly set, but is not yet
fully hardened.

Cerisettes

Cerisettes belong to the classics in the history of chocolates. They are
cherries (*cerises* in French), complete with stem, which are dipped
into fondant sugar and subsequently coated with chocolate. If the
fondant sugar is processed correctly, it will slowly dissolve into the
liqueur in the fruit and liqueur and sugar will interact. After a few
days, an alcoholic sugar syrup is created in and around the fruit,
within the chocolate shell.

Ingredients

Attractive fresh cherries · 24½ fl. oz (700 g) kirsch, cognac or whisky · 10½ oz (300 g) pure alcohol · fondant · liqueur juice · chocolate sprinkles

Preparation

Wash the cherries in cold water, drain and place in sealable jars. Pour a mixture of kirsch, cognac or whisky with pure alcohol (suitable for food) over the cherries until fully covered. Carefully seal the jars with a cover and keep them for at least one month in a dark place.

Method

Drain the cherries. In the meantime, slowly heat the fondant to a temperature between 120°F/50°C and 140°F/60°C (no more, no less!) while stirring. Dilute the fondant with a little liqueur juice until it forms a thick mass. If the fondant is too thick, coating the fruit will be difficult; if the fondant is too liquid, the sugar layer around the fruit will be too thin.

Hold the cherry by the stem and dip it into the warm fondant.

Immediately place the dipped fruit on wax-free (parchment) paper or on a non-stick mat and leave to cool. If the fondant is heated correctly, it will immediately harden around the fruit.

Finishing touches
In order to prevent leakage, it is a good idea to first provide the cerisettes with a chocolate bottom. To this end, spread a thin layer of chocolate on the bottom using your finger.
As soon as it is fully hardened, carefully dip the entire fruit into the tempered chocolate and then into the chocolate sprinkles.

Chocolate and wine

Chocolate and "pralines" are a sheer indulgence with a cup of coffee or tea, which everyone will agree with. What is a lot less known is that the right combination of chocolate and wine leads to highly desirable sensations. Chocolate – and especially dark chocolate – has a positive impact on health if it is consumed in small quantities on a daily basis. This also applies to red wine, which promotes healthy heart and blood vessels. The combination of both leads to a pleasant and happy experience.

There are an infinite number of variations in the flavor of various chocolates. Just as the type of grape determines the wine's flavor palette, the origin of the cocoa bean largely determines the flavor of the eventual chocolate. Those interested in learning about grapes and cocoa beans will constantly discover new challenges and flavor-enhancing experiences. Combinations of wines and chocolates from across the world will regale the culinary adventurer with delightful flavor combinations. Just sample a few types of chocolate together with a good glass of Port wine, an experience you will not be likely to forget!

The possibilities are endless. Each type of chocolate and every wine have their own specific properties. Tastes differ and invariably lead to discussion. Here we provide a number of scrumptious suggestions, but do not be afraid to experiment!

Fortified wines, such as Port, Sherry and Madeira, are at the top of our list, but we could also be tempted by a Canadian Icewine, a Greek Vinsanto or an Australian Muscat.

Milk chocolate is excellent with distinctly fruity, sweet wines, both red and white. But dry white and red wines also go very well with chocolate as they often contain aromas that encourage the tasting of a specific type of chocolate.

For dark chocolate, the options vary from a dry red wine to Madeira Bual, Malmsey, Port (LBV or vintage) or a Spanish Pedro Ximenes, ideal with chocolate with high cocoa content.

In our opinion, the Fonseca Port wins by a hair over the French Rasteau, but the Madeira scores better in terms of harmony. And combined with chocolate with the highest cocoa content, the Don PX 1967 by Bodegas Toro Albala is just a bit stronger than the Bual Madeira.

But no matter how many tips we provide, the message is to try and taste for yourself. Fully enjoy a journey through a wondrous world of exquisite flavors.

Chocolate cream pie

For ingredients and working method for the chocolate crumble pastry, see *Apricot pie* on page 50.

Chocolate cream ingredients
10½ oz (300 g) cream • 1¾ oz (50 g) glucose • 9 oz (250 g) dark chocolate

Method for chocolate cream
Bring the cream and glucose to a boil. Pour onto the finely chopped chocolate and blend into a smooth ganache.

Finishing touches
Pour the cream filling into the crumble pastry, leave to fully cool and garnish to taste.

Chocolate éclairs

Ingredients
7 oz (200 g) water • pinch of sugar •
pinch of salt • 1¾ oz (50 g) butter •
5½ oz (150 g) flour • 5 to 6 eggs

For the filling
chocolate custard or cream •
chocolate

Method
Bring the water, sugar, salt and
butter to a boil.
Add the flour and keep stirring until
the pastry turns dry. Remove from
the heat and add the eggs one by
one.
Pipe the puffs onto a non-stick tray or a slightly greased and floured
baking tray.
Bake for approximately 20 minutes at 390°F/200°C.
After cooling, cut a small opening in the side and pipe in the
chocolate custard or cream. Coat the top with tempered chocolate.

Chocolate mousse

Ingredients
14 oz (400 g) dark chocolate · 3½ oz (100 g) milk · 21 fl. oz (600 g)
cream

Method
Melt the chocolate, bring the milk to a boil.
Blend the milk with the chocolate and leave to cool to below 85°F/30°C.
Beat the cream into soft peaks and fold into the ganache.
Immediately pipe the mousse into
serving glasses.
Allow to cool before serving.

Chocolate soufflé

Ingredients
4½ oz (125 g) custard · ½ oz (15 g)
cocoa powder · 4½ oz (130 g) dark
chocolate · 4 egg yolks · 4 egg
whites

Method
Make custard and leave to cool.
Combine the sifted cocoa powder
and the melted chocolate and add
to the 4½ oz (125 g) custard.

Use a whisk to prevent lumps.

Add the egg yolks.

Beat the egg whites into medium foam and carefully add to the batter without stirring, in order to retain the lightness.

Pipe this mixture into buttered clay molds.

Bake for about 10 minutes in the oven at approximately 390°F/200°C.

Serve hot.

Cocoa

The dry solids produced by the cocoa bean are referred to as cocoa. Firstly, the *cocoa beans* are thoroughly cleaned. The next step involves the roasting of the beans in order for the cocoa flavor to develop. The roasted beans are subsequently removed from their shells (the so-called *cacao pods*), in order to save the pure core. The pods are sold to companies that use them to produce fertilizers or cattle feed.

The purified beans are now broken into small chunks, which are referred to as *nibs* or *cocoa cores*. These nibs are subsequently finely ground, resulting in a dark brown bitter mass, referred to as *cocoa mass* or *cocoa liqueur*. The cocoa mass is solid when it is cold and becomes highly liquid when heated. This happens because, in addition to the dry substances, the cocoa consists of approximately 54% cacao butter. Two-hundred-and-twenty pounds (100 kg) of cocoa beans eventually only produce 176 lb (80 kg) of cocoa mass. The remainder is made up of waste, such as dust, stones and shells.

For the production of cocoa powder, the cocoa mass is heated in a filter press to approximately 195°F/90°C and the liquid cocoa butter is crushed under high pressure (up to 7112 psi or 500 kg/cm²). The solid cake remaining on the filter cloths is finely ground and, depending on the level of crushing, produces the following:

- fat-free cocoa powder (containing a residue of 10 to 12% cocoa butter)
- cocoa powder (containing a residue of 22 to 24% cocoa butter).

The remaining pressed cocoa butter is deodorized through steam distillation or washing and further processed in the chocolate production chain.

Cocoa tree

The cocoa tree (*theobroma cacao*) is demanding in terms of soil and climate. The average temperature must be high and consequently the tree is only cultivated in countries around the equator (between approximately 20° latitude north and 20° latitude south). In addition, the soil should be rich in organic substances. Major production areas include West Africa (Ivory Coast, Ghana, Cameroon and Nigeria), South America (Brazil and Ecuador) and Asia (Indonesia and Malaysia). In addition, a number of tropical countries produce smaller cocoa harvests.

The cocoa tree requires a moist climate and does not tolerate direct sunlight, which is why it always stands in the shade of other trees. It can reach some 50 ft in height and is an evergreen.

The trunk and large boughs can produce between 500 and 1,000 flowers, of which 5 to 8% are pollinated by insects. These flowers then grow into full-fledged cocoa fruits. They mature in four to eight months and can be harvested. Harvesting still takes place manually since ripe and unripe fruits as well as early-stage fruits and flowers grow on the tree simultaneously. One tree produces approximately 5 pounds of beans every year.

Coconut cubes

Ingredients
9 oz (250 g) coconut milk · 1 oz (25 g) invert sugar · 1 lb 2 oz (500 g) chopped white chocolate · 1 oz (25 g) cocoa butter · 7 oz (200 g) grated coconut · dark or milk chocolate (melted, for decoration)

Method
Bring the coconut and invert sugar to a boil. Pour onto the chopped white chocolate.
Leave to cool to approximately 85°F/30°C and fold in the tempered cocoa butter.
Add the (preferably) lightly roasted grated coconut and mix thoroughly.

Pour the mixture into a frame on a non-stick mat and allow to crystallize sufficiently.

Cut the "dough" into cubes in the desired size.

Dip the cubes into dark or milk chocolate and garnish with a little grated coconut on the surface.

Cream of tartar

Cream of tartar or *tartaric acid* is an acid prepared from tartar. It is a colorless crystalline substance used to give an acid flavor to some sweets and soft drinks. It is also used in sugar production to invert the sugar and it is processed in baking powders.

Tartar is obtained from the deposits of potassium hydrogen tartrate and calcium tartrate on the inner walls of fermenting wine barrels.

Cumquats (candied)

The cumquat is a tart citrus fruit that looks like a small elongated orange. This fruit is rich in vitamin C and potassium and can be eaten with its skin. The cumquat originates in southeast India, but is currently primarily cultivated in China and Japan.

Candying is a process whereby the moisture in the fruit's cells is replaced with a saturated sugar syrup, which results in candied fruits and vegetables with enhanced flavor and long shelf life. They also become quite soft and sweet. By fully or partially coating candied goods with chocolate, a balance is created between sweet

and chocolate. The candying principle is quite simple, but does take approximately two weeks. The process consists of soaking the fruits in increasingly concentrated sugar syrup, thereby allowing the syrup to slowly penetrate into the cells.

Ingredients
Depends on the choice of fruits and the desired quantity. The proportions are shown below.

Method
Wash the fruits, cut them lengthwise, subsequently cut the two halves into three to four sections and place them in a jar with sugar and water. Pour 20 fl oz (6 dl) of water for each 2 lb 4 oz (kg) of sugar. Leave the fruits to simmer for approximately 10 minutes on medium heat. Remove the syrup and drain the fruits on a rack.

Weigh the remaining syrup and add 2¼ oz (60 g) sugar for every 3½ oz (100 g) syrup. Bring this syrup to a boil.

Place the drained fruits in a bowl and cover with the syrup. Leave to rest for 24 hours. Cover the syrup (with plastic wrap, for example). Drain the fruits again.

Add ¾ oz (20 g) sugar for every 3½ oz (100 g) of the remaining syrup, bring to a boil and pour over the fruits. Leave to rest a further 24 hours.

Repeat this process for six days by draining the fruits every 24 hours and fortifying the syrup by adding ¾ oz (20 g) sugar for every 3½ oz (100 g) syrup.

On the eighth day, fortify the syrup with 1 oz (30 g) sugar for each 3½ oz (100 g) syrup (instead of ¾ oz or 20 g) and this time leave the fruits to rest for 48 hours.

On the tenth day, fortify the syrup with 1½ oz (40 g) glucose and ¾ oz (20 g) sugar for every 3½ oz (100 g) syrup. Bring the syrup to a boil, and pour onto the fruits. Cover and leave to rest for a further four days.

On the last day, spread the fruits on a rack and leave them to dry for about two days. The fruits can be kept for an unlimited period if they are stored in a jar in a dry place.

Dipped chocolates

These types of chocolates consist of a filling, which is initially poured into a frame or between leveling guides, after which they are cut into specific shapes after hardening. Dipped chocolates must be fully enrobed in chocolate due to their semi-soft filling. In exceptional cases, the top of the filling is kept uncovered, for example, if it consists of marzipan.

Method
Line a tray with plastic wrap or non-

stick parchment paper, or take four leveling guides and place them on a sheet covered with foil.

Pour or spread the desired filling in it. Use a palette knife or a ruler to smooth out the surface.

Allow the filling to harden in the refrigerator until firm and subsequently spread a thin layer of chocolate on the surface. Cut the edges away, unmold and turn over the sheet (the chocolate layer will strengthen the bottom and is required to be able to more easily dip the chocolates).

Use a knife or chocolate cutter to cut out the chocolates. Ideally, a wire cutter is used.

If using a knife, choose one with a sharp thin blade. Place a slat on the filling and first cut strips. Make sure to keep the knife straight. Cut the ganache strips crosswise by applying the same technique.

Dip the chocolates (see *Enrobing/dipping/coating* on page 91).

Diplomat with chocolate sauce

A dessert that is frequently found in patisserie is the *diplomate*, which is always based on custard to which whipped cream is added in order to create an airy cream. The mixture keeps its shape by adding a little gelatin.

Ingredients
12 oz (350 g) custard · 1½ oz (40 g) rum · approximately 5 gelatin sheets · 15¾ oz (450 g) lightly sweetened whipping cream

Method

Make traditional custard and leave to fully cool. Whip the cream into soft peaks and add the rum.

Soak the gelatin.

Press excess water from the gelatin and slowly melt.

Combine the melted gelatin with the custard and fold in the whipped cream.

Pour the "chibouste" (see below) into a buttered and sugared mold, or use a non-stick mold.

Allow to set sufficiently in the refrigerator and unmold onto a dish. Garnish with luscious chocolate sauce.

Ingredients for chocolate sauce

7 oz (200 g) chocolate · 5½ oz (150 g) milk or water

Method for chocolate sauce

Chop the chocolate into chunks.

Cover with the warm milk or water and blend into a smooth sauce.

Since there is always room for improvement, the professionals have also created a version of this delicious dessert, referred to as "chibouste", which is in fact a *diplomate* in which the cream is replaced with Italian meringue, thus making the recipe lighter. Chiboustes come in all manner of flavors and colors, sometimes enhanced with fruit puree.

Enrobing/dipping/coating

For the sake of clarity, we will provide the various professional terms used in this process.

Method for enrobing/dipping/coating
Fill a mixing bowl with tempered chocolate. Make sure the bowl is full in order for the chocolate to stay at this temperature longer and not to thicken as a result of excess crystallization (see *Multiple crystal formation* on page 140). For that same reason, place the bowl on an insulating layer or use an electric melting tray (see page 114).

If you are right-handed, place the centers to be dipped to your left, the chocolate bowl in the middle and a tray lined with wax-free (parchment) paper on the right. If you are left-handed, reverse this set-up.

The chocolates to be dipped must have a thin chocolate bottom in order to slide from the fork more easily.

Before starting, make sure to bring the centers to room temperature. If there is too much of a difference between the temperature of the filling and that of the chocolate, the latter will become dull after hardening. In the worst of cases, the chocolate will even turn grey. It is therefore best to keep the temperature of the filling as close as possible to that of the tempered chocolate. This is obviously impossible for some centers (e.g., buttercream fillings). In that case, ensure that the center is not too cold and still stiff enough to be dipped.

Then dip the filling into the chocolate and cover it completely with the help of a dipping fork.

Slide the fork under approximately two-thirds of the chocolate, allowing for one-third to immediately adhere to the paper (the fork can then be easily removed without the chocolates shifting).

With up and down movements, shake the excess chocolate from the filling, each time gently tapping the chocolate surface with a finger, which will result in a thin chocolate coating.

Remove excess chocolate from the bottom by wiping the fork on the edge of the bowl.

Carefully place the chocolate on the paper.

Gently remove the fork from the chocolate.

Leave the chocolates to harden at room temperature. Do not place in the refrigerator. If the ambient temperature exceeds 75°F/23°C, it is best to first leave the chocolates to slightly set before placing them in the refrigerator (never below 50°F/10°C).

Figurines

Molds

There are two types of molds.

- Single molds: in which the chocolate is poured, cooled and from which it is then removed. Sometimes, two halves must be stuck together (Easter eggs, for example).
- Double molds: consist of two mold halves that are stuck together to form a single mold.

The chocolate is poured into the mold through an opening, then cooled and unmolded (by separating the two halves).

Method

Ensure that the molds are glossy and only handle at room temperature.

Pour the tempered chocolate into the mold and thoroughly agitate the mold in order to remove any air bubbles from the chocolate.

Make sure the entire mold is covered with chocolate.

Turn the mold upside down in order for the excess chocolate to flow back into the chocolate bowl.

Leave the mold to drain for a few minutes on a rack or place on wax-free (parchment) paper. In the latter case, a thicker edge is created, which will subsequently make it easier for both halves to adhere.

When using large molds, ensure that the chocolate layer is thick enough, otherwise the chocolate will break when it is removed from the mold after cooling (in this case, pour a second layer after allowing the first one to slightly set).

Scrape the chocolate remnants from the top of the mold and place the mold in the refrigerator for at least 20 minutes with the open side facing up (if the mold stays with the open side facing down too long, the chocolate could turn grey).

After cooling, the chocolate will have shrunk sufficiently to be removed from the mold. To this end, if necessary, using the back of a palette knife, gently tap on the edge of the mold to release the chocolate. Unmold on a clean table; it is also recommended to wear gloves in order to avoid fingerprints on the chocolate.

Finely ground chocolate

The degree of grinding also helps to determine the quality of the chocolate.

Chocolate producers always finely grind the cocoa mass since no particles should be detected when eating chocolate. The finer the grinding, the more energy required, the more expensive the production process… and the better the chocolate.

The fineness of the cocoa particles is expressed in μm or μ (mu, micrometer or micron; 1μm = 1/1000 millimeters). After final grinding, most particles measure less than 20 μm, but a number of coarser particles are always left behind. Below is an overview of the particle sizes:

Chocolate	Fineness
Very fine	particles < 18 μm
Fine	particles between 18–22 μm
Coarse	particles between 22–27 μm
Sandy	particles > 30 μm

Fondant sugar

Fondant sugar is a white, soft, creamy sugar "dough". If stored properly in hygienic conditions, it will stay soft for several months.

Fondant sugar dough is a semi-finished product that is used fairly frequently by professionals since it is quite cheap when bought in bulk. It is used in patisseries to glaze cream puffs, éclairs and cakes. Chocolatiers turn it into cream to fill chocolate shells.

In small quantities, it is not only hard to find, but it is also more expensive. Fortunately, you can easily make it yourself.

Ingredients
10½ oz (300 g) water • 2 lb 4 oz (1 kg) sugar • 3½ oz (100 g) glucose

Method
Bring water, sugar and glucose to a boil while stirring. Remove the spatula as soon as the mixture boils, as it should no longer be stirred. Clean the rims using a brush dipped in water and place a thermometer in the syrup. As soon as it has reached 240°F/117°C, pour the syrup onto a marble slab between confectionary bars.
Allow the syrup to rest until it reaches approximately 105°F/40°C and knead it using a triangular knife. Keep a palette knife in your other hand in order to regularly clean the triangular knife. In the beginning, the syrup is a very sticky mass, but as the syrup is further processed, it will become opaque and milky. Process the syrup until it suddenly hardens into a solid mass.
Cover with a moist cloth and allow to fully cool.

Cut the cooled dough into pieces and knead briefly resulting in the fondant suddenly becoming soft and creamy. Package the fondant in a box and cover with a lid in order to prevent drying.

Tip If you do not have access to glucose, use the following ingredients: 2 lb 4 oz (1 kg) sugar · 10½ oz (300 g) water · ¹⁄₁₆ oz (3 g) tartaric acid.
The recipe is the same as for glucose; only the cooking temperature differs (250°F/120°C instead of 240°F/117°C).

Frangipane pastry with chocolate

Frangipane ingredients
9 oz (250 g) butter · 9 oz (250 g) powdered sugar · 9 oz (250 g) almond powder · 4 eggs · 2¾ oz (75 g) flour · 1½ oz (40 g) dark chocolate

Method for frangipane
Whip the butter until creamy.
Add the powdered sugar (confectioners' sugar) and almond powder.
Fold in the eggs one by one and thoroughly whip the mixture.
Blend the flour and chocolate into the dough.

Method for pastry
Line a non-stick tray or anti-stick baking mold with a thin layer of puff pastry.

Allow to rest for approximately 10 minutes and cover with a layer of apricot jam. Top with the frangipane to a height of approximately ½ inch (1 cm).

Cut small strips of puff pastry and place them in parallel next to each other on the surface. Repeat crosswise and leave to rest for 10 minutes.

Bake the pastry in the oven between 355°F/180°C and 390°F/200°C. Baking time depends on size and thickness of the frangipane.

Tip   After baking, you could also cover the pastry surface with cooked apricot jam, leave it to set and subsequently add a layer of fondant sugar (see *Fondant sugar* on page 96). Briefly heat the fondant sugar, add a little water to make it more liquid and brush on the frangipane.

Fruit dough with butter and cream

Ingredients
2 lb (900 g) sugar • 10½ oz (300 g) cream • 10½ oz (300 g) glucose • 2 lb 4 oz (1 kg) fruit puree • 5½ oz (150g) butter • 1 oz (25 g) pectin • 3½ oz (100 g) honey • ¾ oz (20 g) water • ¾ oz (20 g) citric acid

Method
Dry melt the sugar and quench with the cream.
Add the glucose, fruit puree and butter.
Continue to cook.

In the meantime, combine the pectin and the honey and add to the mixture. Heat to 225°F/107°C (71°Brix).

Add the citric acid dissolved in water.

Pour the mixture onto a non-stick mat between leveling guides and leave to fully cool.

Cut into cubes and roll in the granulated sugar to finish.

Fruit salad with chocolate cream

Chocolate cream ingredients
5¾ oz (160 g) egg yolks • 4 oz (115 g) sugar • 33¾ fl. oz (960 g) cream • 1 vanilla pod • 3½ oz (90 g) dark chocolate

Method for chocolate sauce
Blend the egg yolks with the sugar until smooth.

Bring cream and sliced vanilla pod to a boil and pour onto the egg yolks. Continue to heat to 185°F/85°C.

Add the melted chocolate.

Fill glasses one-third full with this mixture.

Fruit salad ingredients
1 pineapple • 2 kiwis • 1 mango • strawberries • raspberries

Syrup ingredients
17½ fl. oz (500 g) freshly squeezed orange juice • 5½ oz (150 g) sugar • 1 vanilla pod • 3 cardamom seeds • 1 cinnamon stick • 1 star anise

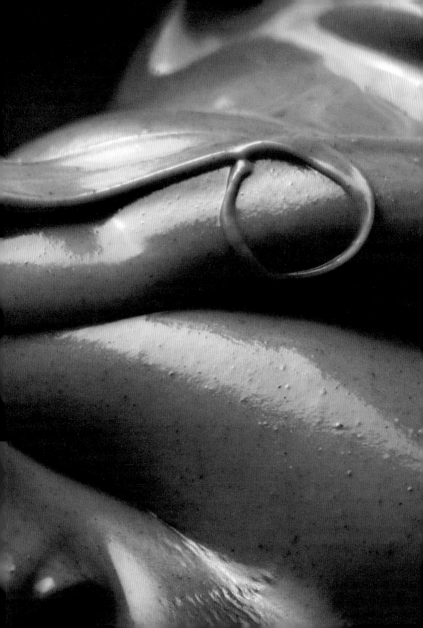

Method for syrup
Bring the juice and sugar to a boil. Add the spices and allow to set overnight. Pour through a pointed strainer.

Finishing touches
Fill the glasses with the fruit salad and cover with the syrup.

Ganache

A ganache is a soft, unctuous chocolate cream, mostly with high-fat content (between 24% and 40% fat). There are 1001 ganache recipes with very diverse applications, e.g., for molded chocolates, cutting chocolates, to use as (chocolate) sandwich spread or to fill and glaze cakes.

The main ingredients in ganache are always fat, water, sugars and dry substances.

In a high-quality ganache, the ingredients must be in perfect balance. The type of fat and its hardness will determine the typical pleasant creaminess expected from a ganache. The dry substances primarily determine flavor and ensure bonding between fat and water. Water will make the ganache lighter.

It is important to create a ganache that meets expectations. Flavor, odor, color and creaminess in the mouth must be in perfect harmony. A high-quality ganache must reflect all of its ingredients and no single ingredient should stand out. If the flavor of one component prevails, the various ingredients are no longer in balance. The art consists in combining the various high-quality ingredients whose aromas complement each other.

Lastly, long shelf life is also of the utmost importance.

Ganache with prunes

Ingredients
3½ oz (100 g) water · 7 oz (200 g) prunes · 1 tsp (4 g) cinnamon
powder · 2¾ oz (80 g) butter · 3½ oz (100 g) honey · 10½ oz (300 g)
white chocolate · 3½ oz (100 g) port

Method
Pour boiling water onto the prunes and leave the latter to swell for
at least an hour in the cinnamon powder.
Puree the prunes in a blender.
Melt the butter. Add the honey and heat until golden brown.
Add the prune puree and leave to thicken to 220°F/105°C.
Pour this mixture onto the finely chopped chocolate or onto the
"Callets" (by Callebaut, a Belgian company) and blend well.
Allow to cool slightly and add the port.
In the meantime, fill chocolate molds with dark chocolate (prepared
earlier).
Allow the ganache to fully cool until it starts hardening around the
edges. Mix thoroughly and immediately pipe into the chocolate
shells. Leave to set sufficiently and seal the molds with chocolate.

Glazing ganache

Ganaches used to cover cakes (glazing) must have an attractive gloss and keep this gloss as long as possible. In order to meet this requirement, we must take into account a number of factors.

The temperature of the ganache compared to the temperature of the pastry to be glazed. It is recommended to first cool the pastry to be glazed.

Precrystallization: It is preferable to slightly precrystallize a glazing ganache. To this end, allow the ganache to rest until it reaches a temperature of approximately 85°F/30°C.

Homogenization: It is best to briefly homogenize the ganache using a hand mixer. The gloss can be improved by making the fat particles as fine as possible. Make sure no air penetrates into the ganache: turn the hand mixer on and off while it is still immersed in the mixture. The following is a recipe for a dark glazing ganache.

Ingredients
1 oz (30 g) gelatin · 10½ oz (300 g) water · 1 lb 2 oz (500 g) sugar · 5¾ oz (160 g) cocoa powder · 5¾ oz (165 g) 40% cream · 2½ oz (70 g) chocolate chips

Method
Soak the gelatin. Combine the water, sugar, cocoa powder and cream. Bring the mixture to the boil and melt carefully.
In the meantime, remove excess water from the gelatin.
Pour the mixture onto the chocolate chips and add the gelatin.

Blend thoroughly. Pour through a pointed strainer.

Heat the ganache between 85°F/30°C and 95°F/35°C and cover the cake.

Honey ganache in molded chocolates

Ingredients

9 oz (250 g) cream · 2¾ oz (75 g) honey · 1 lb 2 oz (500 g) dark chocolate morsels or chips

Method

Bring the cream and honey to a boil and pour this mixture onto the chocolate morsels or chips (e.g., "Callets" by Callebaut).

Stir thoroughly into a smooth ganache. Leave to fully cool.

In the meantime, pour the chocolate molds (see page 136).

Pipe the ganache into the molds to approximately ⅛ inch (3 mm) from the rim.

Leave to set and seal the molds with chocolate.

Place in the refrigerator. Once cooled, unmold.

Imitation or fantasy cocoa

The designations "chocolate" and "couverture" are carefully described in most international Food and Drugs Administration agencies, in which the minimum cocoa component quantities are laid down and allowed sugars and additives are stipulated (see also *Various types of chocolate* on page 180).

In the event of deviations, the designation "chocolate" or "couverture" may not be used and all manner of other terms are introduced, such as fantasy cocoa, cocoa glaze, imitation, coating, etc.

However, chocolate legislation is not the same throughout the world. In a large number of countries, it is permitted to use the term "chocolate" for products with a maximum of 5% vegetable fat other than cocoa butter.

For the designations *imitation* or *cocoa fantasy* (*fantasy cocoa*), there are no restrictions with respect to the choice of ingredients. Hardened fats are used instead of cocoa butter. These products do look like chocolate, but the flavor is obviously less appealing. They can primarily be found in cheaper industrial confections. The advantages of imitation or fantasy cocoa are that the products are cheaper and do not have to be tempered. The disadvantages: the flavor is less pure, fat residue often lingers in the mouth, transfats are harmful to the body and do not stand for quality.

Introduction to the chocolate trade

In order to be able to accurately process chocolate, high-quality equipment is required. But professional equipment is often quite expensive and therefore too much of an investment for those who only occasionally work with chocolate. Hobbyists will typically have to make do with a lot less than professionals. Of course you can limit yourself to the bare bones.

For those who wish to create chocolates, a *special melting tray* is quite handy. Not only can you use it to safely melt the chocolate, but also to keep it at an even temperature for the entire duration of the job.

A *non-stick mat* can be used for both baking and dipping.

Four leveling guides are required to pour a ganache, which, after hardening, can be cut into cubes and dipped into chocolate.

And also:

- a *dipping fork* to coat the confections with chocolate
- a spatula for the melting tray
- a palette knife and a triangular knife
- a sugar thermometer
- wax-free (parchment) paper
- a pastry bag with a number of different tips.

Many professional chocolate equipment suppliers, such as Mol d'Art, put together a kit especially designed for beginners with the most essential equipment at an affordable price. The Mol d'Art set includes a melting tray (7 lb 10 oz/3.5 kg), a dipping fork, a spatula, a palette knife and a cutter.

Invert sugar

Invert sugar (also known under the commercial name Trimoline) is made from regular sugar (sucrose) exposed to acids (lemon juice, tartaric acids) or enzymes, which results in the conversion (inverting) of the sucrose into two components, glucose and fructose, leading to a smaller crystal structure. Invert sugar is a mixture of equal quantities of glucose and fructose (fruit sugar).

A sucrose molecule can be envisioned as a glucose molecule stuck to a fructose molecule. Due to the inversion, the bonding between the molecules is released and creates invert sugar.

Since fructose is sweeter than sucrose, invert sugar has greater sweetening power per ounce than sucrose. Invert sugar is used frequently in the confectionery industry in the production of chocolates, in ice cream and in patisseries: it is processed in products to keep them soft longer. In some cases, it also improves shelf life. It is also used to replace honey, since, from a chemical point of view, honey is mainly made up of invert sugar.

Jasmine ganache

Ingredients
3½ oz (100 g) water · ¼ oz (10 g) jasmine tea · 17½ fl. oz (500 g) cream ·
1¾ oz (50 g) glucose · 1 lb 5 oz (600 g) white chocolate · 12 oz (350 g)
milk chocolate · 2¾ oz (80 g) butter

Method
Bring the water to a boil and allow the tea to brew for 5 minutes.
Bring the cream, glucose and infusion to a boil.
Pour the cream mixture through a strainer onto the white and milk
chocolates.
Leave to fully cool.
Add the softened butter and mix thoroughly.
Cover a chocolate mold with dark chocolate (prepared earlier).
Fill the chocolate shells with the jasmine ganache.
Allow to crystallize slightly and seal the molds.

Lactose

Lactose, or milk sugar, is present in the milk of all mammals.
Therefore, lactose is also present in most dairy products. Although
it typically does not occur in vegetable products, it does in some
tropical plants.

Pure lactose forms large, hard crystals that are difficult to
dissolve. It is not as sweet as sucrose and glucose.

Quite a few people are lactose intolerant. During digestion, lactose is broken down by the lactase enzyme into the monosaccharides of which it is made up. In some people, lactose is not sufficiently broken down due to a shortage of this enzyme. These people are consequently allergic to lactose.

Lecithin

Lecithin is a fatty substance produced from soya beans (for the chocolate industry, among others). It is a completely natural product. Lecithin is also present in egg yolk and in a number of vegetable oils (rapeseed, sunflower seed and corn oil).

In chocolate, the addition of lecithin has a major impact on its fluidity, which is obviously very important to chocolatiers who use it to produce confections and all manner of chocolate products.

Due to its fatty structure, lecithin is soluble in fat and, since water bonds with lecithin, it is used as an emulsifier in chocolate, margarines and mayonnaise (just think of the role of egg yolks when making mayonnaise). It therefore acts as a bridge between water and fat, as it were. In chocolate, it is active around small solid particles (sugar, milk powder and dry substances from the cocoa mass) and helps it to cover them with cocoa butter.

The proportion of lecithin in chocolate varies between 0 and 0.5%. A normal dose for dark chocolate is 0.3%, with 0.5% for milk chocolate.

Liqueur chocolates

If chocolates with liquid liqueur syrup are made correctly, they have a pleasant thin sugar crust, which is not only critical to be able to easily seal the chocolate shells, but also, more importantly to give the chocolates a long shelf life. Alcohol, when in direct contact with the chocolate, affects it and softens it after a while. The confections will lose their gloss and the chocolate layer will collapse, making it look old and unattractive.

Ingredients
1 lb 10 oz (750 g) sugar • 9 oz (250 g) water • 1 oz (25 g) glucose syrup • 2¾ oz (75 g) liqueur or other 60% liquor • 2¾ oz (75 g) pure alcohol approximately 90%

Method
Bring the sugar and water to a boil. Add the glucose syrup, remove the spatula and continue to heat to 220°F/106°C or 225°F/107°C. Do not stir once the syrup boils!
Leave the syrup to cool in a quiet place to approximately 120°F/50°C and add the liqueur and alcohol. Note! Use two bowls to blend the liqueur and alcohol with the syrup (since no stirring is to take place). Pour the syrup onto the liqueur, and immediately transfer to the other bowl. Repeat as often as necessary until you are sure that the ingredients are thoroughly blended.
Immediately cover with household foil and allow to reach room temperature in a quiet place. Avoid vibrations.

Pour chocolate shells. To avoid any undesirable movements, fill the shells with the liqueur at the end of the day to ⅛ inch (3 mm) from the rim (this is best done with a disposable plastic pastry bag fitted with a small tip). Leave to rest overnight in a quiet place.

The following morning, an attractive thin sugar crust will have formed on the surface, allowing the mold to be neatly sealed with chocolate. Since the sugar syrup went from unsaturated to saturated overnight, there is no longer any risk of undesirable crystallization.

Tips   If you do not have access to 60% liqueur, use any other alcoholic drink. The end result will be sweeter and not as strong, however. In order to reduce the sweetness, you can add some salt: 0.03 oz (1 g) of salt should be added shortly before the end of the cooking process. These chocolates should never be frozen.

Macaroons

Ingredients
7 oz (200 g) egg white • 1¾ oz (50 g) sugar• 0.03 oz (1 g) tartaric acid (cream of tartar; see page 85) • 1 lb 1 oz (475) g almond powder with powdered sugar (half and half) • 7 oz (200 g) powdered sugar • 1 oz (25 g) cocoa powder

Method
Beat the egg whites, the sugar and the tartaric acid into peaks.
Sift the almond powder mixture with the powdered sugar and cocoa.

Carefully fold the powder into the foam.

Using a smooth tip, pipe into half-sphere shapes on a Silpat (silicone) mat and bake for 12 minutes in a 300°F/150°C ventilated oven.

Ingredients for the filling
4½ oz (125 g) cream · 1½ oz (40 g) milk · ¼ oz (10 g) invert sugar · ¾ oz (20 g) butter · 7 oz (200 g) chocolate

Method for the filling
Bring the cream, milk, invert sugar and butter to a boil.
Pour onto the chocolate.
Mix thoroughly and leave to fully cool until the ganache starts to set.

Finishing touches
Briefly stir the ganache and pipe between two macaroons.

Magnesium in chocolate

Cocoa is a rich source of magnesium, much more so than green tea or red wine.

Magnesium is a mineral that is essential to the body and provides more energy, increased mental clarity and greater stress resistance. It is said to be crucial to optimal heart function.

Since the body is unable to produce magnesium, it depends on our daily magnesium intake through food.

For example, 3½ oz (100 g) dark chocolate contains approximately 3½ oz (100 mg) magnesium, which represents approximately 34% of the recommended daily allowance (RDA). 3½ oz (100 g) milk chocolate contains approximately 1¾ oz (45 mg) (15% of RDA) and white chocolate approximately ¾ oz (20 mg) (6.5% of RDA).

Manons

Although manons are classics in the history of chocolates, nothing is known about the name's origin. It is possible that the original creator drew inspiration from Massenet's 1884 opera *Manon*.

The manon has undergone a huge transformation throughout the years. Originally, this chocolate had a fresh cream filling that was fortified with butter. Two halved walnuts were placed on the bottom and on the top and the entire confection was coated with fondant sugar. This made this chocolate not only very sweet, but also quite large. The fondant sugar coating had to stay glossy, which required a lot of craftsmanship.

Throughout the years, some changes have been made to the recipe. Since the manon was unstable due to the bottom walnut, the latter was replaced with a layer of marzipan or crunch. In order to distinguish this amended version from the original manon, it was given a new name by many chocolatiers, i.e., the Ben Hur.

This transformation took place not only for practical reasons; the overwhelming sweetness also played a major role, which resulted in the manon falling by the wayside, in particular with the increased popularity of chocolates with lower sugar and fat content. In the meantime, the fondant sugar coating has been replaced with white chocolate, allowing these chocolates to be more easily coated with chocolate.

The original recipe is presented here.

Ingredients
1 lb 2 oz (500 g) butter · 1 lb 2 oz (500 g) fondant sugar (for the filling) · 35 fl. oz (1 kg) cream · vanilla or mocha flavor · walnut halves · fondant sugar (for the coating) · water

Method
Whip the butter until soft, add the fondant sugar and heat slowly.
Add the cream and beat the mixture into butter (i.e., until the moisture starts separating from the fat). In order to make the cream somewhat more solid and extend its shelf life, some of the water is removed in some cases, which is however not a requirement.
Briefly heat the edge of the bowl and beat the cream again until smooth. Flavor with vanilla or mocha.

Cut away any irregularities on the inside of the walnuts to obtain a smooth bottom. Arrange the walnuts on a sheet and cover with the whipped cream piped into ball shapes. Top with a halved walnut with the outside facing up. Allow to set in the refrigerator.

Heat the fondant sugar to approximately 105°F/40°C. Add a little water and stir into the desired thickness. Dip the manons one by one. Do not remove all of the manons from the refrigerator at once in order to prevent the fillings from softening. Keep the fondant sugar white for the vanilla manons and add a little mocha flavoring for mocha manons.

Marzipan

Marzipan is a mixture of almonds and sugar, to which generally nothing else is added. Unfortunately, there is no legislation to stipulate the composition of almond marzipan. As a result, some less than professional manufacturers sometimes produce "almond marzipan", which, however, does not consist solely of almonds and sugar.

The best marzipan is made up of 60% almonds and 40% sugar(s). It is quite soft, due to its high almond oil content, and should not be handled too much, in order to prevent the oil from separating. The sugar mostly consists of sucrose with a little glucose, or invert sugar, fondant sugar and/or a little sorbitol or glycerol.

These sugars each play their role in the marzipan (even though marzipan made solely from almonds and regular sugar (sucrose) is just as delectable):

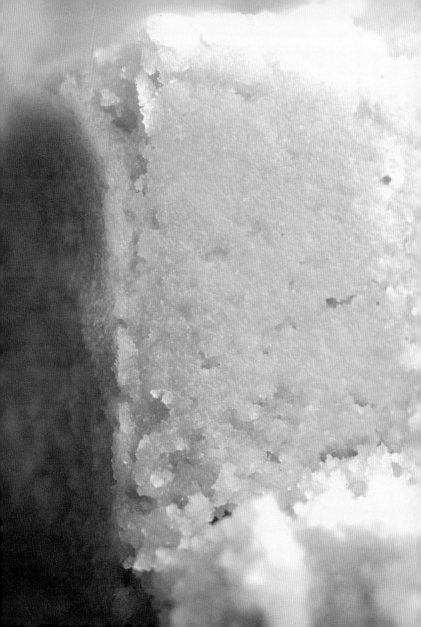

- *glucose* provides the marzipan with a certain elasticity, slows the crystallization of sugar and results in the marzipan drying less quickly
- *invert sugar* slows drying, but is sweeter than sucrose
- *fondant sugar* provides elasticity and easy melting properties
- *sorbitol* ensures that the marzipan dries out less quickly, tastes less sweet and has a longer shelf life
- *glycerol* or *glycerin* has the same effect as sorbitol.

There are two methods for making marzipan: the cold and the warm method.

Cold method ingredients
2 lb 4 oz (1 kg) moist almonds · 1 lb 12 oz (800 g) sugar (can be split, for example, into 1 lb 9 oz (700 g) sugar and 3½ oz (100 g) glucose)

Cold method
Wash the almonds and finely chop them with the sugar(s) in a blender until moist. If desired, add a little water to prevent the oil from separating from the almonds.

Warm method ingredients
2 lb 7 oz (1100 g) broken or crushed almonds · 2 lb 4 oz (1 kg) sugar · 10½ oz (300 g) water · 7 oz (200 g) glucose

Warm method

First, heat the sugar syrup to 235°F/114°C, then carefully add the almonds. Subsequently, chop the mixture in a blender.

Storage

Never cold process marzipan, as this may result in the oil separating; the ideal temperature is 68–70°F/20–22°C.

Preferably store marzipan at a temperature between 50°F/10°C and 59°F/15°C.

Never freeze marzipan.

How to melt chocolate

When chocolate is heated, the cocoa butter contained in it will begin to melt. This takes place from approximately 75°F/25°C. At 98°F/36.5°C, all cocoa butter crystals have disappeared and the chocolate is liquid.

How the chocolate is heated, however, is of the utmost importance. If the chocolate comes in direct contact with a very hot heat source, it will burn. In theory, dark and milk chocolate will begin to burn at approximately 140°F/60°C; white chocolate is much more sensitive and its temperature should never exceed 120°F/50°C.

It is recommended to use a dry heat double-walled melter. A warm water bath is also possible, but is actually not as good for the chocolate. If water or vapor comes in contact with the chocolate, it will thicken and become unsuitable for use in confections. It can, however, still be processed in creams.

It is also possible to melt chocolate in the microwave, but this has to take place in steps. Turn on the oven for short periods of time and regularly remove the bowl in order to thoroughly stir the chocolate (to prevent burning). If you proceed carefully, you can even temper the chocolate immediately after melting and therefore have it ready for processing. To this end, it is best to remove the bowl from the microwave every 10 seconds, as soon as the chocolate begins to melt, and continue to stir until you notice that the last hard morsels no longer seem to melt. The cocoa butter crystals that are still present in these particles are now used to "seed" the

melted portion. In any case, first take a sample on a knife tip (see also *Tempering* on page 164) before processing the chocolate.

Milk powder

Milk powder gives milk chocolate and white chocolate a specific flavor.

For the production of milk powder, the water is removed from the milk, leaving only the dry substance in the milk. This powder is produced in two different forms: *fat-free milk powder* (based on skim milk) and *whole milk powder* (based on whole milk). Depending on the desired chocolate flavor, you can use fat-free milk powder, whole milk powder, or both in various proportions.

The production method for milk powder also plays an important role in the preparation of chocolate. We distinguish spray-dried milk powder, roller-dried milk powder and milk crumb. The production of milk crumb takes place according to a special drying process whereby sugar is added to the milk, which is evaporated and vacuum dried, resulting in a very fine caramel-like and creamy flavor.

Nutritional value of milk powder per 3½ oz (100 g):

	Fat-free milk powder	Whole milk powder
kcal	349	66
kJ	1460	274
water	4.0 g	88 g
protein	35 g	3.7 g

Mocha delight

Ingredients
14 oz (400 g) cream · 1¾ oz (50 g) glucose · 1 ½ oz (40 g) finely ground coffee · 2¼ oz (60 g) honey · 2 lb 12 oz (1,200 g) milk chocolate · 7 oz (200 g) butter

Method
Bring the cream, glucose, coffee and honey to a boil.

Pour the liquid onto the melted chocolate and leave this ganache to cool to room temperature. Blend the softened butter into the ganache. Spread the mixture in a frame and place in the refrigerator for about 10 minutes.

Cover with a thin layer of dark chocolate. Cut the sides away from the frame, unmold and turn over.

Using a round cutter, cut out circles approximately 1 inch/25 mm in diameter. Just knead the "refuse" back together and place between confectionary bars between two wax-free papers. Using a rolling pin, roll out the filling evenly.

Dip the ganache chocolates into dark chocolate (previously prepared). Garnish.

Moelleux without flour

Ingredients

9 oz (250 g) dark chocolate • 3½ oz (100 g) butter • 3½ oz (100 g) egg yolk • 8 oz (225 g) egg white • 1¾ oz (50 g) sugar

Method

Melt the chocolate and blend with the butter.

Add the egg yolks to the mixture.

Beat the egg whites and the sugar into soft peaks and carefully fold into the batter.

Pipe the batter into anti-stick molds and place in the freezer for one hour.

Bake for approximately 8 minutes in a 390°F/200°C oven. Remove the molds from the oven when the cake's edges start rising.

In order to be able to unmold the moelleux more easily, it is recommended to briefly place it in the freezer.

Serve on a dish, covered with a ganache and garnish with finely steamed fruit cubes on the side.

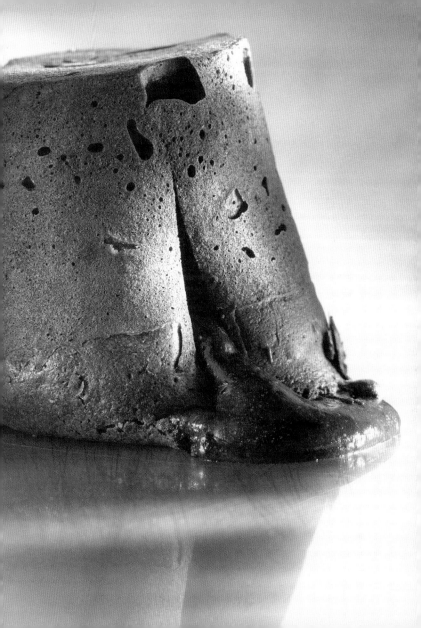

Montélimar nougat

Ingredients
1 egg white • 3½ oz (100 g) sugar • 9 oz (250 g) honey • vanilla •
1 lb 2 oz (500 g) roasted almonds

Method
Firmly beat the egg white with the sugar.
Boil the honey to 275°F/135°C. Pour the honey onto the egg whites
while stirring and heat to 240°F/116°C.
Add the vanilla (to taste) and the almonds.
Pour the nougat into a frame on a Silpat (silicone) baking mat or on
rice paper. Allow the nougat to cool; cut and package the chunks (or
dip them into chocolate).

How to mold or pour chocolates

To this end, molds are obviously needed. Molds used to be made from
metal, but these days they are made from synthetic material, which is
much cheaper than metal and provides the chocolate with a higher
gloss. The best molds are made from polycarbonate.

Molded chocolates can be used for a lot of different fillings, as long
as the latter can be piped. In order to be able to easily fill the molds,
a soft, more or less liquid substance is required, such as ganache or
liqueur-, fondant- sugar- and praline-based fillings.

The more liquid the filling, the smaller the mold should be, since
nothing is more annoying than a dripping filling.

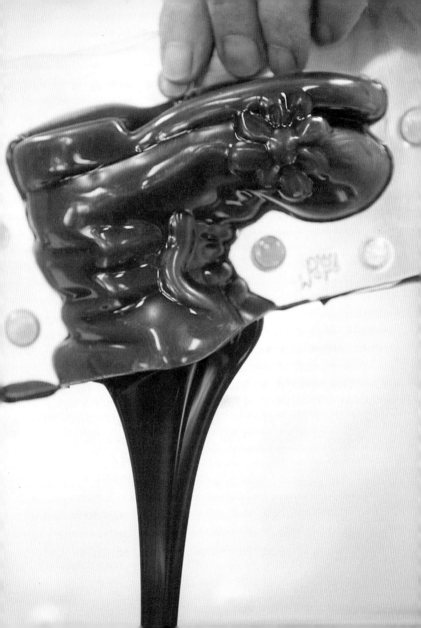

Method

Fill the mold with tempered chocolate, while keeping it slightly inclined in order not to coat all sides. Using a palette knife, scrape the excess chocolate from the mold's outside and outer edges.

Thoroughly agitate the mold on the worktop in order to remove the air bubbles from the chocolate.

Turn the mold upside down, allowing the excess chocolate to fall back into the chocolate bowl. This will leave a thin layer of chocolate in the mold. This chocolate layer should not be too thin, since otherwise the chocolates will either break or not separate from the mold later.

Using a palette knife, scrape all the excess chocolate from the rim and sides of the mold and place on paper to set. After a few minutes remove the mold from the paper. Once again smooth out the surface and place the mold in the refrigerator for approximately 5 minutes with the opening facing up.

Now fill the mold with the filling of your choice. To do so, it is recommended to use a pastry bag fitted with a smooth tip. Fill to $\frac{1}{16}$ inch (2 mm) from the top, otherwise it will subsequently be impossible to close the mold. Allow the filling's surface to set. Using a palette knife, apply a small quantity of chocolate and smooth out the surface. Scrape off the excess chocolate from the rim and place the mold in the refrigerator for approximately 30 minutes (never in the freezer!). Make sure to unmold properly. Quickly but carefully turn over the mold onto a clean sheet of paper. Lightly tap the mold with the back of the palette knife to release the chocolate.

Muffins

Ingredients
7 oz (200 g) dark chocolate · 2¾ oz (75 g) butter · 2 eggs · 10½ oz (300 g) milk · 5½ oz (150 g) sugar · 7 oz (200 g) flour · 1¾ oz (50 g) almond powder · ⅛ oz (5 g) baking powder

Method
Melt the chocolate and fold in the butter. Subsequently, add the eggs, milk and sugar.
Blend the flour with the almond powder and baking powder.
Pipe the dough into a non-stick muffin pan or into paper cups. Bake for 20 to 25 minutes in the oven at approximately 355°F/180°C.

Multiple crystal formation

If the chocolate is correctly tempered (see *Tempering* on page 164), it will contain the correct quantity of cocoa butter crystals required to provide the chocolate with an attractive gloss, shrinkage (required for all manner of molded shapes) and hardness.

If you process tempered chocolate properly for some time, it will slowly begin to thicken, even if kept at its processing temperature. This is caused by the over-crystallizing of the chocolate and implies that once the chocolate contains a number of crystals, the latter will automatically start to multiply, resulting in the chocolate developing too many crystals and thickening. This process will continue if no action is taken. Some professionals believe that, in this case,

additional cocoa butter must be added to make the chocolate more liquid, but that is incorrect. It provides a stopgap solution, but subsequently the problem is aggravated and the thickening process speeds up, since the cocoa butter in the chocolate crystallizes.

When chocolate thickens after tempering, two options can reverse this process:

- briefly heating the chocolate and ensuring that not all crystals are melted
- introducing a small quantity of untempered chocolate into the thickened chocolate.

If you merely continue to work with over-crystallized chocolate, problems will occur. In the best of cases, the chocolate will be less glossy after setting, but the risk is great that it will turn gray and that the chocolate layer will also be much thicker than normal.

Nest made from flour-free cake

Ingredients
2 oz (55 g) water · 2⅜ oz (65 g) sugar · 5½ oz (150 g) dark chocolate · 3½ oz (100 g) softened butter · 2 eggs · 1¼ oz (35 g) sugar

Method
Bring the water and 2⅜ oz (65 g) sugar to a boil. Pour onto the chocolate. Add the butter.
Beat the eggs with the remaining 1¼ oz (35 g) sugar into firm peaks. Carefully fold the foam into the ganache. Divide this mixture into round molds.

Place the molds in a water bath and bake at 285°F/140°C for approximately 40 minutes (until the top feels firm).

Place the molds with their contents in the freezer for approximately 2 hours. Unmold by slightly heating the outside.

Garnish to taste.[3]

Nibs

Nibs are the cleaned, disinfected, roasted, ground cocoa cores sifted to size. These cocoa cores are quite bitter as they contain no sugar. They are ideal for a composition to balance sweet and tart. These hard particles, furthermore, contribute to a pleasant crunchy product.

---

[3] The decoration on the photo is achieved by piping chocolate strips onto frozen marble, removing them immediately from the marble slab, shaping them into circles thus creating a nest and placing it on the cake (for further details, see my book *Chocolate Decorations* (2007).)

Ouzo truffles

Ingredients
7 oz (200 g) cream · 5½ oz (150 g) glucose · 2 lb 4 oz (1 kg) dark chocolate · 5 oz (140 g) Ouzo · 7 oz (200 g) butter · chocolate flakes (to finish)

Method
Bring the cream and glucose to a boil. Pour onto the chocolate and add the Ouzo. Leave to fully cool.

Fold in the softened butter and mix thoroughly. Using a smooth tip, pipe this filling into elongated strips or oval shapes on fat-free paper. Allow to set in the refrigerator. Divide the long strips using a knife. Dip the pieces into dark chocolate (previously prepared) and roll in chocolate flakes immediately afterwards.

Ouzo is a Greek anise-based liqueur. Other anise liqueurs are obviously also suitable provided they only contain a small amount of sugar.

Tip In some cases the ganache separates. Should this happen, it

should be left to slightly set on the bowl's surface and edges while cooling. Subsequently blitz into a smooth mass in the food processor. Pipe out immediately.

Bread paste

This tasty chocolate paste will keep for at least one month, if stored in a cool place.

Chocolate paste ingredients with dark chocolate
5½ oz (150 g) dark chocolate · 7 oz (200 g) butter · 1 can (approximately 14 oz (400 g)) sweetened condensed milk · 1 oz (30 g) cocoa powder

Chocolate paste ingredients with milk chocolate
7 oz (200 g) milk chocolate · 7 oz (200 g) butter · 1 can (approximately 14 oz (400 g)) sweetened condensed milk

Method
Beat the tempered chocolate with the butter into a smooth cream. Add the sweetened milk (and the cocoa powder). Blend until the chocolate paste is smooth. Immediately pour into jars and seal.

Pastry with nuts

Ingredients
10½ oz (300 g) butter · 11½ oz (330 g) sugar · 4½ oz (130 g) flour ·
1 vanilla pod · pinch of salt · 2¾ oz (80 g) finely chopped hazelnuts · 1¾ oz (50 g) finely chopped walnuts · 5 eggs · 6 oz (170 g)
dark chocolate

Method
Melt the butter and blend with the sugar.
Add the flour, the seeds from a cut vanilla pod, the salt and the nuts.
Beat the eggs and add them to the dough. Blend thoroughly.
Add the chocolate and beat the batter.
Pour the batter into a non-stick cake mold.
Bake for approximately 50 minutes at 390°F/200°C.
In the meantime, puree apricot pulp in a blender and bring to a boil.
Place the cake on a rack to cool.
Cover the warm cake with the apricot puree.
Then pour the ganache over the cake (see *Glazing ganache* page
109).

Pizza dough with chocolate (for savory fillings)

Ingredients
12 oz (350 g) flour · pinch of salt · 1 table spoon olive oil · 7 fl oz
(2 dl) water · ½ oz (15 g) yeast · 5½ oz (150 g) dark chocolate

Method

Combine the flour, salt and olive oil. Add the water with the dissolved yeast. Fold in the melted chocolate. Knead the dough for 5 minutes. Work into a ball and leave to rise for 15 minutes.

Remove the air from the dough and divide into two equal pieces. Roll out both pieces into thin sheets.

Place the pizza crusts on a lightly greased baking sheet or on a non-stick mat and cover with the filling of your choice. Leave to rise for a further 20 to 25 minutes. Bake for about 10 to 15 minutes at approximately 435°F/225°C.

Plessis-Praslin

The old spelling for the word "praline" was "prasline" and dates back to 1662. The delicacy is named after Field Marshal Plessis-Praslin. His chef, Lassagne, thought of frying an almond in a little boiling sugar and the "prasline" was born, which was spelled "praline" *after 1680*. Here, we present the recipe for the very first "praline".

Ingredients

1 lb 12 oz (800 g) sugar • 7 oz (200 g) water • 1 lb 2 oz (500 g) almonds or hazelnuts • ¹⁄₁₆ oz (2 g) tartaric acid dissolved in ¼ oz (10 g) water • coffee flavoring to taste • coloring to taste

Method

Bring 3½ oz (100 g) water and 14 oz (400 g) sugar to a boil.

Stir the almonds (or hazelnuts) into this syrup to allow the latter

to caramelize around the nuts. Continue to heat in order to slightly roast the nuts and caramelize the sugar.

Pour the mixture onto a non-stick mat and leave to cool. Ensure that the nuts do not stick together.

Bring the remaining sugar, water and tartaric acid to a boil, add coloring and flavoring to taste. Stir well and continue to heat.

Immediately pour the mixture onto a non-stick mat and leave to fully cool before packaging.

A second layer of sugar is not really necessary, and some professionals only work with a single layer. A single, thicker sugar layer lowers the end product's overall cost.

Professional terminology

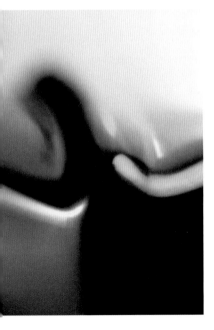

The professional terms often used by chocolatiers are not always clear to everyone. A lot of the terms are borrowed from the French language. Here follows an overview of the most frequently used terms.

What is referred to in Belgium as a *praline* is typically called a *bonbon* in the Netherlands; different terms are often used between countries, or the same terms have a different meaning.

Coating sweets or bonbons with chocolate is referred to as *dipping* in Belgium, although some professionals prefer the term *enrobing*. In the Netherlands, this is referred to as *coating*, *glazing* or *covering*.

As regards the molding of chocolates, we professionals agree on the language; we say that the chocolates or bonbons are *molded*. Exceptionally, we will hear that they are *shaped*.

Different terms are used for the process that treats the melted chocolate to make it easy to work with and to achieve a good end result. We mostly refer to the *tempering* or *perfecting of chocolate*. In the Netherlands, they also often refer to *tabling*. The most accurate term is *precrystallizing*.

Spreading chocolate on a stencil to create chocolate decorations, for example, is simply referred to as *stenciling*.

A *ganache* is a moisture-rich chocolate cream (see page 105).

A *Silpat* mat is a trade name, but is actually a non-stick baking mat. It can be used in the oven and tolerates temperatures of -40°F/-40°C to 480°F/250°C. A Silpat mat is also ideal for rolling out dough.

An interesting effect is achieved by *dabbing* the chocolate. This means dabbing the still liquid chocolate using a brush or sponge, resulting in a pointy structure.

Sometimes we *cover* a cake or biscuit with apricot jam to prevent drying: we apply apricot puree boiled with sugar to the cake using a brush.

Custard or *crème pâtissière* is often erroneously referred to as pudding. Currently, the designation *crème anglaise* is also used regularly.

The term *pudding* originates in England and has a much broader meaning there than in Belgium. A Yorkshire pudding, for example, contains meat fat and an original Christmas pudding is rich in candied fruit, raisins, apples, suet, brown sugar and spices. It is made six weeks in advance to reach its optimal flavor.

In Flanders, (bread) pudding is considered to be a pastry made from old bread, eggs, milk, sugar and raisins.

Quetzalcoatl

When the Aztecs occupied the current valley of Mexico in 1300, they founded a new empire that extended to the border with the Mayas, who believed that their god Quetzalcoatl had donated the cocoa tree to humanity. He also taught them how to make the drink "Cacau". This drink was a foamy mixture of cocoa, ground corn, honey, some *Pimenta Officialis* (a type of Indian pepper) and other spices with water. In Nahuatl (the Aztecs' language), it was referred to as "Cacahuatl", which literally means "bitter drink". The ground cocoa, "chacau haa", would later become "chocoatl". This is how cocoa acquired a symbolic as well as a commercial value.

Quiche with pears

Dough ingredients
3½ oz (100 g) flour • 1 oz (30 g) ground almonds • 2¼ oz (60 g) butter • 2¼ oz (60 g) milk

Ingredients for filling

14 oz (400 g) half pears in syrup (from can or carton) • 1¾ oz (50 g)
butter • 1¾ oz (50 g) sugar • 2 eggs • 3½ oz (100 g) ground almonds •
½ oz (15 g) cocoa powder

Method

Combine the flour and the ground almonds, add the butter and
knead into a crumbly dough.

Add the milk and beat into a smooth dough.

Cover the dough and leave to set in the refrigerator for
approximately 15 minutes.

Roll out the dough evenly and use it to line a buttered mold.
Puncture holes in the bottom using a fork in order to prevent air
bubbles.

Preheat the oven to 390°F/200°C.

Drain the pears.

Whip the butter and the sugar; add the eggs one by one, ground
almonds and, lastly, the cocoa powder.

Pour this mixture into the dough mold. Spread the pear halves on
the surface with their round side facing up and gently press them
into the mixture. Bake for approximately 30 minutes.

Leave to cool and sprinkle with a little powdered sugar or spread
thickened pear juice on the surface.

Raisin ganache

Ingredients
3½ oz (90 g) raisins • 2¼ oz (60 g) cognac (60°) • 12 oz (350 g) cream •
1 lb 7 oz (650 g) milk chocolate

Method
Soak the raisins in the cognac overnight.

Puree the raisins in a blender.

Bring the cream to a boil and melt the chocolate.

Pour the cream onto the melted chocolate and add the puree.

Leave the ganache to cool to approximately 75°F/25°C.

Briefly stir the ganache and pour it onto a non-stick mat between
four leveling guides or into a frame.

Leave to set sufficiently and then cover with a thin layer of dark
chocolate to create the bottom (see page 89).

Now leave to fully set, then turn over and cut using a knife or
chocolate cutter.

Dip into dark chocolate (see page 91).

Garnish.

Raspberry

Ingredients
5¾ oz (160 g) raspberries (or raspberry puree) • 7 oz (200 g) sugar •
5½ oz (150 g) glucose • 10½ oz (300 g) cream • 2½ oz (65 g) butter

Method
Puree the raspberries in a blender. Caramelize the sugar with the
glucose until the mixture turns an attractive light golden brown color.
Carefully quench the mixture with
small quantities of cream, add the
butter and boil briefly.

Carefully add the puree and heat
back to 230°F/112°C.
Leave to cool. Fill chocolate molds.
After the chocolate has set, pipe the
cooled cream into chocolate shells
to approximately ⅛ inch (3 mm)
from the rim.
Leave to crystallize sufficiently
before sealing the molds with
chocolate.

Raspberry jam with chocolate

Ingredients
4 lb 8 oz (2 kg) raspberries (or puree) • 1 lb 12 oz (800 g) sugar • juice of 1 lemon • 9 oz (250 g) dark chocolate

Method
Combine the raspberries with the sugar and lemon juice and simmer for approximately 5 minutes. Fold in the chocolate and continue to boil to 220°F/106°C.
Fill jars with the jam.

Refractometer

The refractometer is an optical instrument that provides a simple, fast and accurate measurement of dry components in sugar-containing syrups such as jellies, fruit syrups and some fillings. It determines the light refraction index[4] for a solid (or liquid) substance, is easy to handle and is frequently used in the confectionery, dairy and the pharmaceutical industries. Its unit of measurement is the *Brix*.

Its smaller version, the pocket refractometer, is a very handy aid for chocolatiers. Be careful when purchasing this tool, since there are refractometers for thin syrups (from 0 to 50° Brix), for thick syrups (from 45 to 82° Brix) and for all syrups (from 0 to 90° Brix).

---

[4] Light changes direction as it moves from one environment to the next. The angle between incoming and outgoing light is the breaking index.

Sachertorte

In the 19th century, the Viennese Sacher family, who owned several hotels, created a type of luxury chocolate cake: the *Sachertorte*. Here we provide the recipe for this by-now world famous cake.

Ingredients
3½ oz (100 g) butter · 3½ oz (100 g) powdered sugar · a little vanilla · 2¾ oz (80 g) egg yolk · 1 egg · 3½ oz (100 g) almond powder · 4½ oz (125 g) dark chocolate · 1½ oz (40 g) flour · 3½ oz (100 g) egg white

Method
Whip the butter with two-thirds of the powdered sugar and the vanilla. While stirring continually, add the egg yolks, the whole egg and then the almond powder. Melt the chocolate, blend it into the mixture and carefully fold in the flour. Beat the egg white with the reserved powdered sugar into foam and carefully fold into the batter (without stirring).
Pour this mixture into a greased and floured mold (or a non-stick mold), and bake in the oven at 355°F/180°C.

After cooling, coat the top and sides of the cake with apricot jam. Cover the mixture with a glazing ganache (see page 106).

Saffron ganache

Ingredients
14 oz (400 g) cream • 3 oz (85 g) honey • 0.04 oz (1 g) saffron • 1 lb 10 oz (750 g) white chocolate • 1½ oz (45 g) butter

Method
Bring the cream, honey and saffron to a boil.
Pour the mixture onto the chocolate through a strainer and leave to cool.
Add the softened butter and mix thoroughly.
Pour the mixture into a frame and allow to set.
Cut to the desired size and coat the chocolates with tempered milk chocolate (see *Tempering*, below).
Garnish to taste.

Tempering

Tempering is aimed at making the chocolate glossy and hard. We often hear that it is quite difficult to make chocolate glossy and to achieve a solid layer. Nothing is further from the truth, as long as you know what happens to chocolate while it is being processed.

Cocoa butter: the main component in chocolate

If you examine good quality hard chocolate under a microscope, you will see an image of cocoa butter crystals, which neatly fit together. Since they are so neatly organized, the chocolate is hard and glossy, just like chocolate from the chocolate factory.

If you want to create something with chocolate, the latter must obviously first be melted. But this results in the structure of neatly arranged fat crystals being melted and the cocoa butter to become liquid in the chocolate. If you just leave the melted chocolate to cool, it will frequently turn gray, have a grainy appearance and remain quite soft.

What to do to achieve a good end result?

Special treatment is needed. In professional circles, the term *tempering* or *perfecting the chocolate* is used for this process. Many people are under the erroneous impression, however, that this means that the chocolate must be brought to a specific temperature. We must indeed try to recover the cocoa butter crystals, but the use of a thermometer makes little sense here.

For clarification, we will draw a comparison with butter, since the hardening behavior of butter is more or less the same as that of chocolate. (Warning! This example is for illustration purposes only; cocoa butter cannot be replaced with butter, but the crystallization process is more or less the same.)

Attractively hardened and shiny chocolate, just as butter, is the result of the correct crystallization of fat. The fat in chocolate is cocoa butter.

The following comparative diagram will clarify a number of aspects.

BUTTER	CHOCOLATE
Fresh butter melts in the mouth since it consists of microscopic fat crystals.	Chocolate also melts in the mouth, since it consists of microscopic fat crystals.

MELTING

Butter turns into oil. (All crystals are melted.)	Chocolate becomes liquid. (Most of the time all crystals are melted.)

REHARDENING

The oil turns into a grainy and unpleasant butter. Appearance and flavor are unattractive. (Now there are large irregular fat crystals.)	See above. The chocolate turns gray and sandy. Lack of gloss and melts very rapidly when touched. (Now there are large irregular fat crystals.)

Remedy
There are three solutions to give butter its attractive smooth and creamy structure:

1) Only melt two-thirds (one-third still contains sufficient crystals to affect the rest).
2) Allow to cool while stirring until slight thickening occurs.
3) Add good (hard) pats of butter until slight thickening occurs.

"Perfecting" chocolate

The simplest way is to melt two-thirds of the chocolate and finely chop one-third. Then gradually add the chopped morsels to the melted chocolate, until the morsels no longer melt easily.

All crystals will dissolve in the melted chocolate, while the finely chopped chocolate will remain full of the crystals required to achieve the correct gloss, hardness and shrinkage in the end product. Chocolate is sold in drops for this purpose in stores.

Method

Stir a small portion of the chopped chocolate into the melted chocolate.

- If the chocolate chips melt easily, this implies that the chocolate is still too hot. Add some more chips until you notice that they no longer melt easily when stirred.

- If the chips do not melt at all, this means that you have added too many chips (and therefore crystals). This will not enable you to do a good job, since this chocolate will rapidly begin to thicken. In this case, you will have to carefully heat the chocolate to dissolve the last remaining unmelted morsels. Note that if too much heat is applied, the crystals will melt as well and you will have to add more chocolate morsels.

Test   In order to ensure that the chocolate is good for use (in other words, that the right crystals are present), you can either insert the tip of a knife into the chocolate and put it aside, or pour a small quantity (e.g., a few drops of chocolate) onto paper. If the chocolate starts setting within a few minutes, this indicates that the chocolate is tempered and can now be processed. You can start the job and have fun with the chocolate.

Tip   If during processing the chocolate starts to thicken slightly, this means that once again too many crystals are forming and it is best to carefully heat the chocolate, as described above. In this way you can keep the chocolate ready for processing for hours (see page 140).

Theobroma cocoa

Theobroma cacao is the scientific name for the cocoa (tree), and comes from the Greek *theos* (= god) and *broma* (= spice), which together means *godly spice*.

Cocoa is produced from the cocoa fruit. The *cocoa pod* – as the fruit is called – is oval, 6 to 10 inches (15 to 25 cm) long and approximately 2¾ to 4 inches (7 to 10 cm) thick. Depending on the variety, the fruit turns green, yellow, yellowish red, red and eventually reddish brown as it ripens. The shell is ¼ to ⅞ inch (5 to 20 mm) thick. The fruit contains 25 to 30 beans, which are embedded in a jelly-like pulp. The beans or cocoa cores are very rich in fat; they contain an average of: 54% cocoa butter · 11.5% protein · 9.5% organic acids and natural flavorings · 9% cellulose and raw vegetable fibers · 6% tannins · 5% moisture · 2.6% minerals and salts · 1.2% theobromine · 1% carbohydrates · 0.2% caffeine.

Topic-type bar

Ingredients
3½ oz (100 g) grated coconut · 10½ oz (300 g) coconut liqueur (e.g., Batida de Coco) · 10½ oz (300 g) butter · 10½ oz (300 g) fondant sugar · 1 lb 10 oz (750 g) milk chocolate

Method
Soak the grated coconut flakes in the liqueur.
In the meantime, lightly whip the butter.
Add the fondant sugar and continue to stir the mixture.
Add the chocolate. Then the coconut liqueur and flakes.
Spread out large drops of milk chocolate on a sheet lined with wax-free paper. Immediately shake the sheet in order to create chocolate circles measuring approximately ⅞ inch (20 mm) in diameter.

Pipe the butter ganache into pointed peaks onto the bottoms using a pastry bag fitted with a star tip. Allow to set sufficiently and dip into milk chocolate (see page 91).

Transfer sheets or silk-screened foil

Silk-screened foil is a shiny foil printed with colored cocoa butter and is used to give the surface of chocolates a decorative appearance. This method of decorating is also often used for special occasions. For example, businesses or associations can provide their clients or members with personalized chocolates. There is even a special printer with food-quality ink with which you can quickly create silk-screened foil for special occasions, such as birthdays.

The principle is simple: by placing the foil on tempered chocolate, the impression stays on the chocolate surface after it has hardened.

For dipped chocolates, place a sheet on the still-liquid chocolate immediately after dipping. In order to guarantee optimal gloss, leave the sheet on the chocolate as long as possible.

Special molds are available for molded chocolates, consisting of two halves. Place a sheet on the bottom and position the other half of the mold fitted with built-in magnets, in order to keep both sections together. Then fill the mold the traditional way.

Truffles

Traditional Belgian truffles have a distinctive round or oval shape. They are usually rolled in cocoa powder, chocolate shavings or almond shavings, immediately after dipping.

Butter truffle ingredients
5½ oz (150 g) butter • 9 oz (250 g) fondant sugar • 3½ oz (100 g) dark chocolate

Method
Beat the softened butter in the food processor until smooth. Add the fondant sugar to the butter in small quantities while stirring.
Fold the tempered chocolate into the butter mixture.
Using a pastry bag fitted with a smooth tip, immediately pipe the cream in the shape of a ball onto a non-stick mat or wax-free paper.
Allow the balls to develop a crust for a half day in order to prevent the chocolate layer around the truffles from cracking.
Dip into tempered chocolate (see page 91).
Then immediately roll in cocoa powder.

Tuiles with cacao nibs

Ingredients
8 oz (230 g) sugar • ⅛ oz (5 g) pectin • 3½ oz (90 g) milk • 6¾ oz (190 g) butter • 3½ oz (100 g) glucose • 10½ oz (300 g) cocoa nibs

Method
Combine the sugar and the pectin.
Heat the milk with the butter and the glucose.
Pour, while stirring – at a temperature of approximately 120°F/50°C – the sugar and pectin mixture into the milk and continue to heat to 230°F/110°C.
Remove from the heat and add the nibs.
Pour the mixture onto a Silpat (or other anti-stick) mat and bake for approximately 10 minutes in a 355°F/180°C oven.

Vanilla

Vanilla is the dried legume of a tropical climbing vine, the vanilla plant. The finest quality vanilla is Bourbon vanilla.

Vanillin is the flavoring that develops after the vanilla's extensive fermentation process. Since the natural supply of vanillin is considerably smaller than its demand, most vanillin is produced synthetically and is a cheap industrial substitute for vanilla. The majority of the world's vanillin production is derived from lignin, a by-product of the paper pulp industry. It is also, to a lesser degree, extracted from the bark of the clove tree.

Various types of chocolate

Since the quality and flavor of cocoa beans depends on various parameters, slight differences in flavor occur, which is why beans from various countries of origin are mixed for most types of chocolate. These blends are necessary to guarantee consistent flavor.

But not all types of chocolate are produced on the basis of cocoa and bean mixes from various areas of origin. So-called *chocolate of origin* is produced from a single cocoa variety. Since an increasing number of consumers are in search of special, authentic flavors, chocolates of origin certainly meet that need. The demand for chocolate of origin is on the rise and the range is ever increasing.

Each cocoa variety has its own properties and specific flavors, which are determined, among others, by the region, the soil and the climate conditions in which it is cultivated. For example, one cocoa variety has typical floral notes, while another has spicy notes.

In chocolate of origin, the intention is exactly to emphasize the aromas of that unique cocoa variety, just as in grand cru wines.

Do note that, just as with wine grapes, the cocoa bean harvest differs from year to year, in both yield and quality, which implies that even chocolate of origin can produce different flavors from year to year. The name of the country of origin is primarily used as the name for the chocolate.

The latest trend among chocolate manufacturers – aimed at marketing an exclusive top chocolate – is to secure an annual contract with a family plantation, most often somewhere far away in the tropics, in order to buy the full harvest in exclusivity.

Viscosity and yield value

It is important for chocolatiers to use chocolate that is most suitable for the relevant application. Often concepts such as viscosity and yield value are cited. These terms are sometimes erroneously interchanged, which leads to confusion. We will provide concise descriptions of both concepts.

Data about *viscosity* provide a good idea about the fluidity of chocolates during processing. Chocolate with high cocoa butter content is more fluid than chocolate with less cocoa butter. Viscosity describes fluid behavior under **shear stress** (stirring, shaking, etc.).

Yield value describes chocolate fluid behavior under *minor stress*, such as flowing **under its own weight**. The degree of grinding of the chocolate is especially important. Very fine chocolate is less fluid than very coarse chocolate. More cocoa butter must be added to fine chocolate to achieve a fluid behavior that is comparable to that of coarse chocolate with less cocoa butter. This concept is, for that matter, also used in the paint industry. If you have painted a wall and the paint drips, i.e., flows under its own weight, you are dealing with a paint with a low yield value.

White chocolate mousse with goat cheese

Ingredients
6 oz (175 g) white chocolate • 1¾ oz (50 g) mild goat's cheese • 2¼ oz (60 g) butter • 3 eggs • 3½ oz (90 g) sugar

Method
Melt the chocolate and blend it with the goat's cheese and butter in the food processor. Separate the eggs. Add the egg yolks to the mixture one by one and continue to blend until smooth.
Beat the egg whites with the sugar into a semi-firm foam.
Carefully fold the foam into the chocolate mixture without stirring. Do not blend any longer than necessary in order not to lose the foamy texture. Fill the glasses with the mousse and briefly place in the refrigerator before serving.

Xocoatle

Xocoatle is the name of the chocolate drink as it was prepared some 4,000 years ago by the inhabitants of a small village in the Ulua valley in Honduras. This drink was prepared

and drunk in mugs. From the remnants of the oldest settlement found by scientists there, it appears that this drink was prepared in the mugs from which it was also drunk. This location is now considered to be the "cradle of chocolate".

Yin-yang

Ingredients
2 lb 4 oz (1 kg) butter · 1 lb 2 oz (500 g) fondant sugar · 9 oz (250 g) kirsch · 4 lb 8 oz (2 kg) milk chocolate

Method
In preparation, pipe drops of tempered chocolate onto a sheet of wax-free paper. Thoroughly shake in order for the drops to spread open. These chocolate circles will serve as the bottoms for the yin-yang chocolates.

Soften the butter and add the fondant sugar. Beat into an airy cream. Fold in the kirsch and the tempered milk chocolate.

Immediately pipe the cream into sphere-shaped peaks on the chocolate bottoms with the help of a smooth-tipped pastry bag. Leave to set and subsequently dip into dark chocolate (see page 91).

To finish, carefully dip the point of the confection into the chocolate and immediately afterwards into the powdered sugar.

Zenith

Ingredients
3½ oz (90 g) red berries • 3½ oz (100 g) cream • 1 oz (30 g) honey • 1 lb (450 g) milk chocolate

Method
Puree the berries in the blender.

Bring the cream and honey to a boil, add the red berry puree and return to a boil.

Leave to fully cool and strain onto the tempered chocolate.

Pour the mixture onto a non-stick mat between four leveling guides or into a ½-inch (10-mm) frame and leave to fully crystallize.

Cover with a thin coat of dark chocolate to serve as a bottom.

Turn over and cut to the desired dimensions, using a knife or chocolate cutter.

Dip into dark chocolate (see page 91) and garnish.